Jack the Ripper

Jack the Ripper

ANDREW COOK

AMBERLEY

First published 2009

Amberley Publishing
Cirencester Road, Chalford,
Stroud, Gloucestershire, GL6 8PE

www.amberley-books.com

British Library Cataloguing in Publication Data.
A catalogue record for this book is available from the British Library.

ISBN 978 1 84868 327 3

Typesetting and Origination by Amberley Publishing.
Printed in Great Britain.

CONTENTS

PRINCIPAL CHARACTERS

Inspector Frederick Abberline	Scotland Yard Inspector seconded to H Division
Sir Robert Anderson	Assistant Commissioner, Metropolitan Police
Supt' Thomas Arnold	Head of H Division (Whitechapel)
Wynne Baxter	Coroner, Country of Middlesex, Eastern District
Frederick Best	Freelance Reporter, *Star* newspaper
Dr Thomas Bond	Police Surgeon to Commissioner
Dr Frederick Brown	Police Surgeon, City of London
John Brunner	Proprietor of the *Star*
Thomas Bulling	Journalist, Central News Agency
Annie Chapman	Murder victim, died 8 September 1888
Dr Percy Clark	Assistant to Dr Bagster Phillips
Frances Coles	Murder victim, died 8 February 1891
Louis Diemschutz	Discovered body of Elizabeth Stride
Catherine Eddowes	Murder victim, died 30 September 1888
Sir James Fraser	Commissioner, City of London Police
Mary Kelly	Murder victim, died 9 November 1888
Joseph Lawende	Witness in Catherine Eddowes case
Chief Inspt' George Littlechild	Head of Special Branch, Scotland Yard
George Lusk	Chairman, Whitechapel Vigilance Committee

PRINCIPAL CHARACTERS

Sir Melville Macnaghten	Assistant Chief Constable, Metropolitan Police
Inspector James McWilliam	Head of CID, City of London Police
Henry Massingham	Assistant Editor, *Star* newspaper
Henry Matthews	Home Secretary
John Moore	Manager, Central News Agency
Thomas P O'Connor	Editor of *Star* newspaper
Ernest Parke	Journalist, *Star* newspaper
Dr Bagster Phillips	Police Surgeon, Whitechapel
John Piser	Bootmaker known as 'Leather Apron'
Inspector Edmund Reid	Head of CID, H Division, Whitechapel
Israel Schwartz	Witness in Elizabeth Stride case
Emma Smith	Murder victim, died 3 April 1888
Major Henry Smith	Acting Commissioner, City of London Police
Elizabeth Stride	Murder victim, died 30 September 1888
Chief Inspt' Donald Swanson	Headed Whitechapel murder investigation
Martha Tabram	Murder victim, died 7 August 1888
Sir Charles Warren	Commissioner, Metropolitan Police

PREFACE

120 years after he terrorised the streets of Whitechapel, 'Jack the Ripper' continues to fascinate us. Over 200 books, 5 feature films and nearly 200,000 web pages retell the story of London's favourite murderer.

The Ripper is part of British folklore blended seamlessly with the world of Sherlock Holmes, hansom cabs and thick grey fog. Somehow, this perverted slum murderer has become a figure of mythical proportions.

He is the archetypal bogey man, a shadowy figure in a top hat and opera cloak stalking the mean streets of London's East End. Even now, 120 years on, everybody recognises that image as 'Jack the Ripper'. The Ripper was not caught and no-one can be certain who he was, so how and why was the popular vision of Jack the Ripper actually created?

We owe Jack the Ripper to the pioneering editors and unscrupulous hacks of the Victorian press, the great grandfathers of tabloid journalism who understood that murder sells papers. This is the story of how the popular press faked evidence, printed fantasy and mislead the police investigation in a ruthless pursuit of shocking headlines.

London in 1888 was a bustling port and a hive of industry at the heart of an enormous and prosperous empire, ruled over by an ageing Queen Victoria. Not everyone, however, was reaping the rewards of imperial and industrial success.

In the East End the lower classes endured extreme poverty and degradation. London society was clearly divided between the haves in the West End and the have-nots in the East End.

In the East End people didn't have enough to eat, they didn't have decent places to live, there was no proper sanitation, cheap gin was the crack or heroin of the day, and many were hopeless drunks. The industrial era had brought with it a climate of lawlessness and social deprivation, which in turn gave rise to innumerable crimes, some of them deadly, whose perpetrators could merge back into the swarming urban population. The newspapers provided a focus for public fear and morbid fascination in this criminal underworld, and as they still do, they made a mint out of it.

The creation of Jack the Ripper was the ultimate act of PR genius. It created a macabre national fixation and a figure that has since passed into legend. The truth is almost certainly different. While there were similarities between the murders, the evidence is difficult to square with the theory of a single killer. More than any other newspaper, the newly launched *Star* led the way during the reporting of the Whitechapel Murders, and was the first to push the single killer story. Now, with access to newly available source material on the *Star*, its journalists and management, it is now possible to discover why a newspaper made the ground breaking move from reporting news to creating it. In doing so they inadvertently gave birth to a pseudo-historical myth that has perplexed the minds of historians, amateur detectives and delusional conspiracy theorists for over a century.

Four years ago, during the research for what eventually became the book *Cash for Honours*, I first came across the name of John Brunner. Although political corruption was a key ingredient of the book and one of the honours touts, Arthur Maundy Gregory, was rumoured to have been involved in the mysterious death of Edith Rosse in 1932, the nature of the research was hardly bedded in the mire of the criminal underworld.

Seeking out the many heirs and descendents of those ennobled during the premiership of David Lloyd George was a mammoth task. It was one made even more remarkable by the number of those who were happy to provide access to family papers and records irrespective of whether or not they suspected their ancestor of purchasing privilege.

The scope of the research became even more daunting when it became apparent that Lloyd George was merely continuing a policy of systematically selling honours that had begun under his predecessor Herbert Asquith. The scope of the search was therefore taken back a decade, and that's when Brunner's name first came to light on a list of potential recipients written in 1911 by Alick Murray, Asquith's Chief Whip.

Although Murray had developed an effective network of touts to tap-up potential recipients of honours and steer their cheques in his direction, Brunner, through his membership of the House of Commons, was already known to him as a man of wealth and position who might be worth approaching. When, in 1911 it appeared that the House of Lords might reject the Government's Parliament Bill, aimed at curtailing their power to veto legislation, Asquith, not without some difficulty, managed to gain the consent of King George V to create as many as 400 new peers should the Bill be voted down. In this eventuality the newly ennobled warriors would take up the cudgels and force the Bill through the Upper House. As it turned out, the mere rattling of the patronage saber proved enough to concentrate the minds of the Upper House and ensure the Bill's safe passage.

Not everyone in Downing Street, however, was happy with the Lords' surrender. Chief Whip Murray had already drawn up a list of potential new peers and a good many of these worthies were apparently ready and waiting with open cheque books for word from the Chief Whip's office that the mass ennoblement was to proceed. Some of the names on Murray's shortlist were, apparently, not susceptible to the lure of ermine. Awarded a baronetcy by Lord Rosebury in 1895, Brunner considered this an award of merit. Alick Murray's suggestion of showing one's appreciation 'in the usual way' for a peerage very much went against the grain to a man who had worked his way up from a junior clerk at the John Hutchinson & Co. Alkali works in Widnes to General Manager, during which time he had established a deserved reputation for being a paternalistic employer and a man of personal integrity and honest dealing. In 1873 he founded Brunner, Mond & Co. which developed through mergers into the multinational giant ICI.

Brunner was certainly a very wealthy man. According to his July 1919 *Times* obituary, he 'rejoiced in using his wealth for philanthropic ends'. In Cheshire alone, according to his own records, he funded schools, guildhalls, social clubs and libraries across the county. He also donated money to the Liberal cause, usually in connection with certain initiatives or policies, with which he identified or supported, as opposed to blanket donations to party funds. Ensuring that radical Liberal policies were given a fair hearing in the press was a particular concern of Brunner's and to this end he helped fund and found a number of newspapers to ensure that the Conservative press were not given a free reign.

While the storm over the 1911 Parliament Act quickly blew over, for Murray, new clouds quickly descended upon him, for within less than a year he had to flee the country to avoid having to testify before a Parliamentary Enquiry into the Marconi 'insider-dealing' share scandal. That had already engulfed several other senior members of the Cabinet, including the Chancellor of the Exchequer and the Attorney General. Murray, as it turned out, had not only profited himself by buying 1,000 shares, but had also bought an additional 3,000 shares with Liberal Party funds. Again, Brunner spoke out against this breach of trust. Not only was he a principled exception to the many self-made men who characterised this era of political corruption, but as it turned out, an inadvertent conduit to an intriguing mystery I had first encountered some three decades earlier.

In August 1972, I had read a series of articles by former Chief Superintendent Arthur Butler of New Scotland Yard concerning the so-called 'Jack the Ripper' murders. Although Butler's articles were based essentially on undisclosed sources and were somewhat off the mark in terms of their conclusions, he raised several important issues concerning how many of the victims had actually been murdered by the same individual and how the whole notion of a character named 'Jack the Ripper' had caught the public imagination in the first place.

Two decades before his clash with Alick Murray, Brunner had, as a principal shareholder in the Newspaper Publishing Company Ltd (publishers of the *Star* newspaper) became embroiled in a series of head to head disagreements over journalistic standards with Terence Power O'Connor, the company's managing director and editor of the *Star*. As we shall see in due course, O'Connor, who was to play a key role in the creation of the Jack the Ripper myth was a wily operator and in many ways the antithesis of Brunner.

In 1870, three years before the founding of Brunner, Mond & Co., a twenty-two year old T.P. O'Connor arrived in London from Athlone in his native Ireland. According to his own gilded version of events, he had four pounds in his pocket, which represented his entire savings. Already having a fascination for politics and the power of the press, he then apparently set off to see Fleet Street and the Houses of Parliament before looking for a room to lodge. This he found in Catherine Street, off the Strand, conveniently located half way between his twin fascinations.

Determined to find a job in Fleet Street, O'Connor made twice daily raconteurs around the streets and side streets that housed the Victorian newspaper industry. Never one for lacking trepidity he resolved to visit every newspaper office listed in *Kelly's Directory* until he found a position, any position that would get him on the first rung of the newspaper ladder.

One such visit to the *Daily Telegraph* in Peterborough Court resulted in an interview with Levy Lawson, the editor/proprietor. With the war between Prussia and France having recently broken out, and the siege of Paris about to begin, news from the continent was now very much in demand. The *Telegraph's* regular correspondents were sending very little and it seemed possible they might soon be sending nothing at all. Faced with a potentially fatal news draught, Lawson hit upon the idea of gathering news from the French, German, and Austrian newspapers and quickly translating them into English copy ostensibly as the dispatches of *Telegraph* correspondents in France.

Having graduated four years previously with a BA in History and Modern Languages, the Irishman was able to present himself as able in both French and German. Taken on initially for a week's trial in September 1870, O'Connor's first piece for the *Telegraph* was an account of the arrival at Hastings of the Empress Eugenie. The next was a description of the German victory at Sedan and the Emperor's surrender.

Jack the Ripper

With the beginning of the bombardment of Paris on 4 January 1871, the siege of the capital entered a new phase. The Prussian shelling lasted some twenty-three days, usually from two to five hours at a time. As a result the French asked all foreigners to leave the city. Few news correspondents left in the capital had the desire to remain amid the daily danger and uncertainty. With news from Paris now reduced to a trickle, O'Connor hit on a new idea. Encouraged by his success at translating articles, he now ventured to become a little more daring. With Lawson's connivance and a secondhand copy of *The Sights of Paris in Watercolour*, he proceeded to write articles purporting to be from the *Telegraph's* lone correspondent in besieged Paris. Offering dramatic visual descriptions gleaned from the book and from his imagination, he pieced together the few remaining scraps of news that had seeped through from the city and the accounts in French and German newspapers, stringing them into stories about life under siege.

Nearly two decades later, as editor of the *Star*, O'Connor was again to shape and re-cast the news, not this time in a series pastiche pieces from a foreign war, but now in a politically motivated campaign in the East End of London, on the very doorstep of Fleet Street itself, that would leave a far greater imprint on history, well beyond anything he or indeed any other Victorian journalist ever dreamed possible.

CHAPTER 1

WITH THANKS TO

JACK THE RIPPER

The power of the press was something T.P. O'Connor believed should be used unsparingly. In 1888, London had thirteen morning and nine evening national daily newspapers, of which the *Star* was the newest addition. Launched in January 1888, O'Connor saw the paper as a vehicle, not only for his own ambitions but equally for a new style of journalism. Evening papers had traditionally been priced at a penny per copy. O'Connor's *Star* pitched in at a cover price of a halfpenny, aiming at a lower middle-class and skilled working-class readership, that thanks to the 1870 Education Act were becoming literate in ever increasing numbers.

Although circulation figures for the newspaper industry during this era are scant and somewhat open to question in terms of accuracy, it is undeniable that the *Star* made an immediate and striking impact on its target audience from day one. Never one for veracity or false modesty, O'Connor proclaimed on the paper's masthead, printed before the first copy had even been sold, that the *Star* had the 'Largest Circulation of Any Evening Paper in the Kingdom'. Although the *Evening News* had a far greater claim to that boast in January 1888, thanks to O'Connor's combative stewardship of the paper during those first crucial months, his claim would soon become a reality.

Jack the Ripper

Along with W.T. Stead of the *Pall Mall Gazette*, O'Connor was one of the leading evangelists of the 'new journalism', a revolutionary approach to the communication of news that was in many ways the forerunner of today's tabloid red-tops both in terms of style, approach and content. Stead, who had been editor of the *Gazette* since 1883 saw editors as the, 'uncrowned kings of an educated democracy' and understood that the working man did not want dry broadsheets full of parliamentary reports. He made his paper unashamedly entertaining, scandalous and bold. He pioneered investigative journalism by buying a thirteen-year-old virgin in order to expose the ills of child prostitution. Looking today at the headlines Stead employed in this particular series of campaigning articles, such as 'Confessions of a Brothel Keeper' and 'Strapping Girls Down', we see the close correlation with today's tabloid sensationalism. As a result of publishing this story, Stead received a three month prison sentence on the grounds that he had failed to first secure the permission for the 'purchase' from the girl's father. While the price he paid was a high one, the story made a massive impact and the *Pall Mall Gazette* sold out day after day. As a consequence, the government was pressurised into bringing forward legislation to raise the age of consent to sixteen.

O'Connor too was a man with a political agenda, although unlike Stead he had no scruples whatsoever when it came to achieving his ends. Almost from the moment he arrived in London, he made no secret of the fact that his twin ambitions were to become both a Member of Parliament and the editor of a major newspaper. When, towards the end of his life O'Connor wrote his memoirs, he undoubtedly glossed over or conveniently forgot the political chicanery which led to him winning a parliamentary seat in 1880. If he had any party allegiance whatsoever it was to the

Liberal Party, where he was very much on the radical wing. In the two years prior to the 1880 election he had cultivated the Liberal MP Sir Charles Dilke with a view to gaining his assistance in securing a nomination in a winnable Liberal seat, ideally one with a radical membership.

Many of the radical constituencies were to be found in the north of England but only one of these, Dewsbury, had shown even a modicum of interest in short-listing O'Connor. A confidential letter written by Irish Parliamentary Party MP Timothy Healy to Party Leader Charles Parnell on the eve of the 1880 election provides a unique insight into O'Connor's Damascus like conversion to the Irish Party. Apparently O'Connor had made covert overtures to Healy about the possibility of an Irish seat on the collapse of his last hopes of securing the Dewsbury nomination. 'I think that O'Connor is politically a Liberal above all and .... would become a Home Ruler if he could not be a Liberal. He might be very useful to us as a speaker and writer. Try him with Home Rule'. Despite O'Connor's initial luke-warm attitude to Home Rule and his opposition to the Roman Catholic Church's political influence, he gladly accepted Parnell's terms. As a result Parnell ensured O'Connor's selection for the Irish constituency of Galway City, which he won with a knife-edge majority thanks to a going rate of £40 per vote and the decisive support of twenty-four dead men, who despite the limitations of their condition turned out to vote him into office.

After the election, Healy dryly noted that O'Connor 'stood for an Irish seat because he could not get elected for an English one'. Although he had endorsed O'Connor's candidacy, it seems clear that Healy had little liking for the new member for Galway City and was somewhat concerned at the antics he and fellow IPP MP

Phil Callan were to indulge in at Westminster. Together they were allegedly responsible for a number of tricks played on Conservative MPs who resided in a building opposite the Palace of Westminster. There was apparently an underground passage by which the MPs could hurry into the divisions lobbies when they heard bells ring. On one particular night O'Connor and Callan cut the wires of these bells when a division was called. The Conservative Whips waited in vain for the MPs whose votes they had been banking on.

O'Connor was by reputation a great raconteur and a man of great wit and bonhomie. As soon as he arrived at Westminster he immediately set about cultivating Liberal MPs (and indeed anyone of whatever political persuasion) he felt might one day be of use to him. One such individual was Henry Labouchere, the journalist and Liberal MP for Northampton who had also won his seat at the 1880 general election.

With the defeat of the Irish Home Rule Bill in 1886 and the consequent split in the Liberal Party, the Government fell and a Conservative Government under Lord Salisbury took office. By the following year, O'Connor was looking for a new challenge and began to consider the possibility of launching a new radical London evening newspaper. Apart from realising a long held ambition, it seems clear from O'Connor's papers that the timing of this bold move was more than likely motivated by the fact that his finances were now on their beam ends. As a result of a disastrous investment in a cotton and tobacco enterprise in Virginia he had lost every penny he had put in. He was now left with virtually nothing, save his meagre parliamentary allowance and the modest and irregular sums he earned from writing.

With this precarious position being his motivator, idle thoughts soon took on a more practical bent. In July 1887, several months after the investment debacle, he and his wife Elizabeth were holidaying in Brighton with the Laboucheres when O'Connor chanced to mention his idea for a new paper over lunch. Clearly sounding out potential Liberal support for the paper, he was somewhat taken aback to learn from Labouchere that a similar project was already being confidentially discussed within the Liberal Party and that meetings to sound out potential backers had been held the previous week. Quick witted as ever, O'Connor called the Liberals' bluff and told Labouchere that he was not only confident of financial backing but could move his plans forward very quickly should the rival project progress.

Knowing that there was probably not enough room in the market for two similar papers, Labouchere undertook to approach those associated with the other initiative and see if some compromise might be possible. This he did, and during the parliamentary recess of 1887 a series of meetings took place between O'Connor, Labouchere and the two principal backers of the Liberal evening newspaper project, John Brunner and mustard manufacturer William Colman.

The upshot was that Brunner and Colman concluded that their initiative could be dead in the water if O'Connor launched first. O'Connor for his part managed to convince the duo that he and they had a similar purpose and that his paper would provide what they were seeking in a bold and radical alternative to the Tory evening papers. Little did they know he had not two pennies to rub together, let alone launch an evening newspaper. While others were brought in to the consortium, it was essentially the money put forward by Brunner and Colman that made the enterprise a reality.

O'Connor's account of how the *Star* was conceived, written over four decades later is unsurprisingly different. Labouchere and his gallant efforts are airbrushed out of the story entirely. Instead, and true to form, O'Connor paints an entirely different picture:

> I conceived the idea, half in hope, half in terror, that I might start a journal myself in favour of the views of myself and my friends to ask them for the capital, which I placed at £40,000. There was an interesting episode. Two of the richest members of the Liberal Party were brought together by me-they seemed to me to look at each other like two goats preparing for a fight; when one expressed his readiness to subscribe £10,000, the other answered immediately that he would contribute the same; £20,000-half my capital! My joy may be imagined. As a matter of fact, one of them entirely changed his mind and never subscribed a penny; the other, after long negotiation, agreed to subscribe £5000-half the amount he had originally promised. But I got the £40,000; and, much to my subsequent undoing, I got £2000, for the promise of a seat on the board, from a very cantankerous Scotsman, who afterwards contributed to my undoing.
>
> I was innocent as a babe at the time of all things connected with finance or with companies; I didn't realise the importance of getting together a board that might be relied upon to deal in a friendly spirit with me. One member I insisted on putting on out of my warm personal affection and admiration for his great public spirit; he contributed even more than the other to my undoing. I did not realize that he had vast ambitions of his own, and that a great London paper could greatly help him in realising these ambitions; nor how these ambitions could react on his attitude to me.

Despite his reassurances to the contrary, the kind of radical paper O'Connor had in mind was to be totally alien to the straight-laced radicalism envisaged by Brunner and Colman.

In addition to proving the £40,000 necessary to start the newspaper, they also agreed to give Connor £1,200 per annum and a 25 per cent share of any profit made after a cumulative dividend of 5 per cent had been paid to preference shareholders.

O'Connor also negotiated that he should not only be editor of the *Star*, but the managing director of Newspaper Publishing Ltd, the proprietary company created by Brunner and Colman to manage the *Star*. He even managed to have Clause 78 of the company's Articles of Association specially crafted as follows: 'Thomas Power O'Connor, Esq; MP; shall be the managing director of the company, and shall not be removable except by a special resolution' passed by a three-fourths majority of the shareholders. Brunner and Colman, while not entirely happy with this, ensured that Clause 70(B) allowed the board of directors to 'appoint any one of more of their number to be managing director, or managing directors.' In other words, if they could not remove O'Connor as easily as they might wish, they could at least frustrate his ability to run the company by creating a second managing director if necessary. They also ensured that the rest of the board was packed with their own friends and allies and further consoled themselves with the 5 per cent clause, which, Brunner informed O'Connor was 'to protect the preference shareholders from the risk that for some years they should get nothing.'

The omens for a harmonious working relationship between O'Connor and his fellow directors were not good from the very beginning. At the first board meeting on 19 December 1887 he antagonised his fellow directors, James Stuart MP; Richard Eve; Wilfrid Blunt; Briggs Priestly MP; and Charles Schwann MP with a diatribe against obsolete journalism. Giving the board a taste of things to come he distributed a copy of his first draft editorial which was very much a battle cry for the

Opening with a statement bound to ruffle the feathers of the Liberal party stalwarts he declared, 'We believe that the reader of the daily journal longs for other reading than mere politics.' The *Star* would, he went on, 'would do away with the hackneyed style of obsolete journalism,' and signaled that there would be, 'no place in it for the verbose and prolix articles to which most of our contemporaries still adhere.'

Setting the tone for the type of coverage that would later typify the Whitechapel murders, O'Connor emphasised the need to dwell on the 'human side' of reporting stories. Whatever the misgivings of the board, these sentiments not only appeared in the first *Star* editorial but were bolstered by the declaration that:

This is a Radical journal. It will judge all policy, domestic, foreign and social, from the Radical standpoint. This means that a policy will be esteemed by us good or bad as it influences for good or evil the lot of the masses of the people. The rich, the privileged, the prosperous, need no guardian or advocate; the poor, the week, the beaten require the work and word and word of every humane man and women to stand between them and the world.... Empire, dominion, influence in the councils of Europe, all these and suchlike things to us are mere pestilent emptiness. The elevation, the more constant employment, the better wages, the increase of food in the stomach; dignity in the souls; joy humanity, tenderness in the hearts of the people, these are the things alone represent to us progress, glory, national greatness.

The *Star* would, he continued, attack all privilege:

for privilege stands as a barrier on the very threshold of the kingdom into which we would have all sons and daughters of men enter. Privileged degrades alike the man who is and the man is not privileged. The privileged are made selfish from their earliest years, for they are taught to forget the equality in all essentials of all human beings, to demand too much for themselves and to concede too little to others; and privilege equally degrades the poor by cultivating unmanly servility; forgetfulness or the right of every man and women to demand their fullness share of the common fund of happiness that lies within the state; and by suppressing that desire and power to rise to the highest position in the state which is the first necessity of a nation of free, honest and self-respecting citizens. The House of Lords, the property vote, the monopoly of parliamentary life by the rich-these all belong to the edifice of privilege and must be swept away. We hope to help in bringing the day when, as in the United States and in France and in Switzerland, every citizen stands exactly equal before the nation, except in so far as he has been elevated to higher position by the confidence of his fellow-citizens.

In a *New Review* article at the time of the *Star's* launch he declared his belief that:

the public has suffered more from the cowardice than from the audacity of journalism, from the suppression rather than the publication of awkward facts… everything which can be talked about can be written about.

O'Connor's uncompromising style was also evident in the way he assembled and managed staff of the *Star*. For some months before the paper's launch he had been interviewing potential journalists at the offices Brunner and Colman had acquired for the *Star* in Stonecutter Street, off Ludgate Circus.

First among the recruits was Henry Massingham, formerly of the *Eastern Daily Press* and *Norfolk News*, who was appointed assistant editor. Ernest Parke had rapidly graduated from the *Birmingham Gazette* to Fleet Street's *Evening Echo*, and was recommended to O'Connor by John Robinson of the *Daily News*. Parke was seen as a natural 'new journalist' and was offered the post of chief sub-editor. George Bernard Shaw was appointed as assistant leader writer along with journalist Robert Donald.

Although undoubtedly a rare judge of journalistic talent, according to Robert Donald, O'Connor also had a propensity for foisting friends or persons who asked help of him on firms he worked for. This tendency is particularly evident in the recruitment of freelance staff that included theatre critic Arthur Walkley, literary columnist Clement Shorter and jobbing reporters Frederick Best and Michael O'Brian.

With his new team assembled O'Connor resolved, 'like the merchants of old London, to live in my place of business', and had the two top floors of the *Star* building converted into a flat, where he and his wife where to live for the next two and a half years. It was here, where according to Elizabeth O'Connor, 'the rooms shook and trembled from the whirring machinery and the air reeked of printer's ink' that O'Connor wrote his first article for the *Star*. 'I wrote it' he later recalled, 'in a white heat; it is, I believe, one of my best articles I have ever written.' The passage he was particularly proud of read as follows:

> The charwoman that lives in St Giles, the seamstress that is sweated in Whitechapel, the labourer that stands begging for work outside the dockyard gate in St George's-in-the-East, these are the persons by whose condition we shall judge the policy of the different political parties, and as it relieves or injures or leaves unhelped their position, shall that policy by us be praised or condemned, helped or resisted.

It was ironic then that a story which would spring from the very area of Whitechapel and St George's-in-the-East would be responsible not only for securing the *Star's* future but for making it the leading evening newspaper. For O'Connor, the Whitechapel murders were a god-send. In fact, when he wrote his memoirs decades later, he entitled the chapter dealing with this particular period, 'Jack the Ripper Helps.' Jack the Ripper, he freely conceded, 'helped to make gigantic circulations hitherto unparalleled in evening journalism.' In a book notable for its embellishment and gilding, this was probably one of the most accurate statements to be found between its covers.

Mary Ann Nichols was initially regarded as the third casualty of an individual killer or a gang, who had been on the rampage for some months before the 31 August 1888. This justified the *Star's* proclamation that 'London lies today under the spell of a great terror', as a 'nameless reprobate, half man half beast, is daily gratifying his murderous instincts'.

To this point, two varied accounts had existed. The first of these ascribed the slaughter to a protection racket run by a gang of 'ruffians'. *The Times* and the *Daily News* published the same story on 1 September, identifying the murderers as a 'High Rip' gang demanding payment from prostitutes, otherwise exacting their terrible revenge. This account was echoed in *The Advertiser* on 7 September, when they reported that the murderers 'make their appearance during the early hours of morning' and 'put away their victims' to prevent the police being informed of any crime. The story was attributed in each case to unidentified police sources. Further colour was added by the *Herald,* maintaining that the gang, 'have been under the observation of the police for some time past'. Furthermore, 'the prospect of a reward and a free pardon' meant that some of its members 'might be persuaded to turn Queen's evidence, when some startling revelations might be expected'.

However, the *Star* took the lead with a different story. Newly established in 1888, supposedly at the forefront of the 'New Journalism', this account accredited the murders to a single assassin. However, in the same way as those newspapers which reported the 'High Rip' gang, the *Star* also claimed its explanation was backed by police sources. Furthermore, it supported its story by conjecturing about the circumstances of the crimes. The following list of evidence was presented to readers on the day of Mary Ann Nichols' killing:

The previous murder of Martha Tabram on 7th August, in which she received 30 stabs, must also have been the work of a maniac. This murder occurred on a Bank Holiday. On the Bank Holiday preceding another woman, Emma Smith, was murdered in equally brutal but even more barbarous fashion by being stabbed with a stick. She died without being able to tell anything of her murderer.

All this leads to the conclusion, that the police have now formed, that there is a maniac haunting Whitechapel, and that the three women were all victims of his murderous frenzy.

The *Star* published a special edition the next day, in which it made an extended argument for the existence of this monster. 'In each case,' it noted, 'the victim has been a woman of abandoned (abandoned and unfortunate were Victorian euphemisms for prostitute) character, each crime has been committed in the dark hours of the morning, and ... each murder has been accompanied by hideous mutilation.' Furthermore, the offences were committed in the small part of town: 'each of the ill-lighted thoroughfares to which the women were decoyed to be foully butchered are off turnings from Whitechapel Road, and all are within half a mile.' With a breezy assurance that would characterise many subsequent conjectures about the case, the newspaper pointed to the obvious conclusion: all three murders were 'the work of some cool, cunning man with a mania for murder'.

The media were undecided as to which story was the most fitting in the initial coverage of Mary Ann Nichols' death. The lone killer theory was preferred by the *East London Advertiser*, in agreement with the *Star*. There were various articles supporting the 'High Rip' gang theory. The *Morning Advertiser* published on 1 September reflected on both options before deciding that the 'more reasonable suggestion' was the protection racket. However, the idea of a single 'maniac' gained the upper hand over the next few days.

On 3 September, the lone murderer theory was supported in W. T. Stead's *Pall Mall Gazette*. *The Times* and the *Daily News* changed their views at this point, declaring that the 'three crimes are the work of one individual', rather than their earlier theory of the 'High Rip' gang. They were supported two days later by the account of neighbourhood fears of this 'mysterious assassin' which appeared in the *Daily News*. The rumours of a criminal gang had all but disappeared within a week of Nichol's murder, to be widely replaced by detailed accounts of a lone killer. The 'High Rip' gang theory was finally consigned to history following the murder of Annie Chapman. The phenomenon of the Whitechapel murderer was by this time alive in the public consciousness.

Despite the fact that the *Daily News* reported both the 'High Rip' gang and the 'Whitechapel maniac' in the days following Polly Nichols' murder, in its earliest report of 31 August, the paper reported her death as no more than a one-off misfortune. However, once the *Star* had broadcast a possible link between the three assassinations, this theory spread quickly.

There is no verification that the police connected the three murders, despite implications that the *Star* was following the police lead. Indeed, they presumed that Martha Tabram was murdered by a soldier, having been stabbed with a bayonet, and Emma Smith died as the result of a gang attack. Likewise, they had no evidence to link the earlier deaths with Polly Nichols' killer.

It seems that the 'maniac' theory published by the *Star* was more popular than the version of events published by its rivals. The Whitechapel murders appeared to provide the spark which allowed the paper to take off commercially. Its sales were described as 'a crude barometer of public interest' in the crimes. The root of this fascination lay in the fact that the *Star* first publicised the idea of a mysterious and bloody assassin. The East End was rife with rumours of evil deeds on the streets.

O'Connor effectively launched the 'Ripper industry' on an enthralled public when he fashioned the story of the Whitechapel serial killer from the deaths of Emma Smith, Martha Tabram and Mary Ann Nichols. The earliest stage of this industry illustrates the fundamental role of mythmaking in the process, as the only thing connecting these women was the overwhelming tragedy of their lives. O'Connor was a fervent believer in the virtues of 'new journalism' and that 'the end always justified the means'. The lone murderer theory provided him with the perfect vehicle for his beliefs and arguably for the greatest news headline of all time.

As a result of the continuous retelling of the Ripper story, a host of omissions, distortions and errors have muddied the waters over the past century. Before we proceed any further in our story, we need to remind ourselves of precisely what occurred 120 years ago; not through the ever growing library of 'Ripper' books, with their cast of a thousand implausible suspects and frequently erroneous claims, but from the actual contemporary records of 1888.

CHAPTER 2

MURDER IN RETROSPECT

One of the hardest concepts to combat when discussing or debating the realities of the Whitechapel murders today is the almost unshakeable mindset that so many now have about the perceived killer and his victims. Indeed the victims themselves, as individuals, had almost been expunged from the story altogether until the 1970s. Although most people know about Jack the Ripper and usually have a pet theory of their own, their actual knowledge is almost always based on misconception and assumption often founded on the impression given in films and by popular mythology. In the same way that concrete evidence now exists to repudiate the theory that President John F. Kennedy died as the result of some elaborate conspiracy rather than by the action of an obscure malcontent lone assassin, the sad fact remains that over seventy per cent of Americans continue to prefer the version served up by films and myth, to the more sobering conclusions founded upon hard fact.

The Whitechapel murders too have, over the past century or more, attracted a small army of conspiracy buffs, pseudo historians and amateur armchair detectives, who between them have created more suspects, theories and 'evidence' than a library of Agatha Christie novels. They have thrived and been assisted in their endeavours by one reality, the profound deficit of real evidence. Because there are so few real clues and so little real evidence, it has provided a field day for those pushing their own pet theories and counter theories. It is very much the classic case of 'reverse research'. Many have started with their own hunch or pet theory and then researched backwards trying to make everything fit their chosen solution or conclusion rather than researching forwards with an open mind. If something along the way does not quite fit in with their theory, it is either air-brushed out, or a counter theory contrived to get around the obstacle or explain away the inconvenient truth.

Equally, the fact that during the period the official police files were closed (1892-1992), a number of documents were either inadvertently destroyed or 'lost', has also fuelled the fires of those pushing conspiracy or cover-up theories. It is therefore important to clarify the situation concerning the official records.

In line with police force practice at the time, the majority of written statements taken by individual officers would have been destroyed at the time the investigation was officially closed along with officers' pocket notebooks, arrest warrant copies, bail records and police station custody records.

The records of the City of London police, who investigated the Catherine Eddowes murder, were destroyed by fire as a result of bombing during 1941. However, contrary to myth, this does not mean that we have no awareness of the City investigation as much of the documentation was copied to the Home Office as the investigation progressed, where they remained un-pillaged and thus survived there virtually in tact.

The records of the Metropolitan police, who investigated all the murders bar the Eddowes case, were kept under the supervision of the Registry at New Scotland Yard until they were publicly released to the Public Record Office (The National Archive) in Kew. However, we know from several archivists who worked at New Scotland Yard that a number of documents were taken and never returned, either by unsupervised visitors to the archive or by police officers themselves, particularly, although not exclusively prior to 1948. The original copy of the file on victim Emma Smith, for example, was taken in its entirety and not returned, disappearing at some point after 1972. Again, much of the Metropolitan Police material was copied to the Home Office, which has ensured that a more or less seamless account of the murders has survived.

Those who investigated the case such as inspectors Edmund Reid and Frederick Abberline have also gone on record to confirm that no concrete evidence of any kind concerning any suspect was ever unearthed during the investigations. Reid, in particular was the most assertive; 'I challenge anyone to produce a tittle of evidence of any kind against anyone. The earth has been raked and the seas have been swept, to find this criminal 'Jack the Ripper' always without success.

A number of senior officers such as Assistant Commissioner Sir Robert Anderson, Assistant Chief Constable Sir Melville Macnaghten and City of London Police Commissioner Sir Henry Smith (who were never directly involved in the investigations themselves) made claims many years later in their memoirs concerning evidence, the number of victims and the identity of the killer. Interestingly, many of their key claims were repudiated shortly after their memoirs were published by the very officers like Edmund Reid who had actually carried out the investigations. They knew for a fact that their former superiors were merely making claims to bolster book sales.

However, it has been the claims of these higher ranking officers who had no involvement in the investigations, that have been trumpeted over the decades and incorporated into Ripper folklore. The more pertinent views of those officers and doctors who personally investigated the murders and took part in the victim autopsies have never received the same exposure. They were often in no position to have memoirs written, or more to the point never sought to profit from their careers once retired. They and their views have as a consequence been forgotten by history, but thankfully not entirely lost to posterity.

As we shall see, opinion among such officers and officials at the time reflected none of the certainty or zealotry articulated by many of today's Ripper followers concerning the number of victims and other key aspects of the murders. Bearing in mind the numerous distortions and embellishments that have occurred over the past century in the telling and re-telling of this story, we should not only return at this point to the unimpeachable contemporary sources but use this opportunity to familiarise ourselves with many of the names and characters who punctuate this complex saga.

The most important contemporary source is without doubt the original Metropolitan police 'Whitechapel Murders' file no. 57885 which comprised three grubby manila folders tied up with pink tape. The first of the folders contained individual case files on eleven murder victims, labelled as follows:

Emma Elizabeth Smith, aged 45, murdered on 3rd April 1888
Martha Tabram, alias Turner, aged 34 to 40, murdered on 7th August 1888
Mary Ann Nicholls [sic] murdered on 31st August 1888
Annie Siffey, alias Chapman, murdered on 8th September 1888

Jack the Ripper

Elizabeth Stride, murdered on 30th September 1888

Catherine Beddowes [sic], murdered 30th September 1888

Marie Jeanette Kelly, murdered on 9th November 1888

Rose Mylett alias Lizzie Davis, murdered on 20th December 1888

Alice Mckenzie, murdered on 17th July 1889

Trunk of a Female, found on 10th September 1889

Frances Coles, murdered on 13th February 1891

The following extracts taken from these files and written by those who were actually there at the time experiencing the events first hand, tell the story far more effectively than anyone else, no matter how skilled a writer they might be.

Emma Elizabeth Smith

Shortly after midnight on 3 April 1888 Smith was seen talking to a man dressed in dark clothes and white scarf. An hour and a quarter later she was attacked in Osborne street as she walked past Whitechapel church. Arriving back at her lodgings between 4 and 5 a.m. she was taken on foot to a London hospital by Mary Russell and Annie Lee and was treated on arrival by House Surgeon George Haslip. She died at 9 a.m. the following morning, 4 April, of peritonitis. The police were not called nor informed of the crime until 6 April when they were contacted by the coroner Mr Wynne Baxter.

According to Inspector Edmund Reid from Commercial Street police station, who filed a report:

The first the police knew of this attack was from the Coroner's Officer who reported in the usual manner on the 6th inst. That the inquest would be held on the 7th inst. Chief Inspector West attended. None of the Pc's in the area had heard or seen anything at all, and the streets were said to be quiet at the time.

The offence had been committed on the pathway opposite No. 10 Brick Lane, about 300 yards from 18 George Street, and half a mile from the London Hospital to which deceased walked. She would have passed a number of Pc's en route but none was informed of the incident or asked to render assistance.

The peritoneum had been penetrated by a blunt instrument thrust up the woman's passage, and peritonitis set in which caused death. She was aged 45 years, 5'2" high, complexion fair, hair light brown, scar on right temple. No description of men.

Edmund Reid Inspr.

A further report by Chief Inspector West was included in Smith's file:

Her head was bruised, right ear torn, rupture of peritoneum. According to statements made by deceased the motive was robbery. Deceased could not describe the men who had ill-used her but said there were three of them, and that she was attacked about 1.30 a.m. on the 3rd, while passing Whitechapel Church. Witnesses Mary Russell, deputy at 18 George Street, Spitalfields; Annie Lee, lodger (these two escorted her to London Hospital); George Haslip and Margaret Hames (lodger at the above address who was last to see her alive.)

Jack the Ripper

Martha Tabram alias Turner

On the night of the Bank Holiday Monday, 6 August 1888, 39 year old Martha Tabram, also known as Turner, had been drinking in the White Swan pub on Whitechapel High Street with another prostitute, Mary Ann Connelly, also known as 'Pearly Poll', and two soldier clients. Evidence provided by Connelly showed that she and Tabram, in company with the two soldiers, had visited several public houses in Whitechapel between 10 p.m. and 11.45 p.m., at which time they separated, Connelly going up Angel Alley with one of the soldiers and Tabram up George Yard with the other.

Tabram's body was seen lying on the first-floor landing of George Yard Buildings, George Yard, by Alfred Crow, a cabdriver, who passed the landing at 3.30 a.m. He later told the inquest that he took no notice of it as he was accustomed to seeing people lying about there and had not stopped to see if the body was dead or alive.

Inspector Ernest Ellisdon and Superintendent Thomas Arnold statement in Tabram's file tells us more about the discovery of the body:

METROPOLITAN POLICE

H Division

10th August 1888

I beg to report that at 4.50 a.m. 7th inst. John Reeves of 37 George Yard Buildings, George Yard, Whitechapel, was coming down the stairs of above Buildings to go to work, when he saw a woman lying on the first floor landing. he called P.C. 226H Barrett (on the beat) who found the woman lying in a pool of blood. – there was no blood on the stairs leading to the landing. P.C. sent for Dr. Killeen, 68 Brick Lane, who attended and pronounced life extinct – there being 30 punctured wounds on the body; the police ambulance litter was procured, and the body removed to Whitechapel mortuary to wait an inquest.

Description, age 37, length 5 ft 3, complexion and hair dark; dress, green skirt, brown petticoat, long black jacket, brown stockings, side-spring boots, black bonnet – all old.

A description was circulated in 116 Infn. 7.8.88 – and the body was photographed same date, but up to the present time it has not been identified.

Two copies of photograph attached.

E. Ellisdon Insp.
T Arnold Supd.

From the statements taken it was observed that the murder had taken place between 2 a.m. and 4.50 a.m. and that given the lapse of time it was possible that she may have met someone else. A further examination of the body identified thirty-nine puncture wounds, most of which were inflicted, according to the doctor with a penknife, but one of which, on the sternum, had been caused by a stronger knife, possibly a dagger or bayonet.

Mary Ann Nicholls [sic]

On the evening of Thursday 30 August 1888, at about 11 p.m. Mary Ann Nichols was seen walking the Whitechapel Road.

At 12.30 a.m. she was seen to leave the Frying Pan public house, Brick Lane, Spitalfields. At 1.40 a.m. that morning she was in the kitchen at 18 Thrawl Street. She informed the deputy of the lodging house that she had no money to pay for her bed. She asked that a place might be kept for her, and left, stating that she would soon get the money.

At about 3.40 a.m., Nichols' body was discovered by Charles Cross, who was on his way to work, at the entrance gates to a stable yard in Buck's Row. This spot was next to 2 Buck's Row and opposite Essex wharf. Cross stopped to look at what he initially thought was a tarpaulin. Robert Paul, also on his way to work, came along and Cross showed him the body.

Not able to see very well in the dark, the two men were not sure whether the woman was dead, drunk or otherwise injured. Concerned about being late for work, they went off looking for a policeman and met PC Jonas Mizen at the corner of Hanbury Street and Old Montague Street.

Meanwhile, beat officer PC 97J John Neil has discovered the body. Inspector John Spratling's report of the same day takes up the story:

METROPOLITAN POLICE

J Division

31st August 1888

PC 97J, Neil, reports at 3.45. on 31st inst. he found the dead body of a woman lying on her back with her clothes a little above her knees, with her throat cut from ear to ear on a yard crossing at Bucks Row, Whitechapel. P.C Neil obtained the assistance of PCs 55.H. Smizen [sic] and 96J. Thain, the latter called Dr. Llewellyn,

No. 152, Whitechapel Road, he arrived quickly and pronounced life to be extinct, apparently but a few minutes, he directed her removed to the mortuary, stating he would make a further examination there, which was done on the ambulance.

Upon my arrival there and taking a description I found that she had been disemboweled, and at once sent to inform the Dr. of it, l[atter] arrived quickly and on further examination stated that her throat had been cut from left to right, two disti[nct] cuts behind on the left side. The windp[ipe] gullet and spinal cord being cut through, a bruise apparently of a th[umb] being on right lower jaw, also one o[n] left cheek, the abdomen had been [cut] open from centre of bottom of ribs a[long] right side, under pelvis to left of the stomach, there the wound was jag[ged], the omentium [sic], or coating of the stomach, was also cut in several places, and tw[o] small stabs on private parts, apparently done with a strong bladed knife, supposed to have been done by some le[ft] handed person, death being almost instantaneous.

Description, age about 45, length 5 ft. 2 or 3 compx dark, hair dark brown (turning grey), eyes brown, bruise on lower right Jaw and left cheek, slight laceration of tongue, one tooth deficient front of upper jaw, two on left of lo[wer] do; dress, brown ulster, 7 large brass bu[ttons], (figure of a female riding a horse and [a] man at side thereon), brown linsey fr[ock] grey wollen petticoat, flannel do, white chest flannel, brown stays, white ch[emise], black ribbed wollen stockings, man[s] S.S boots, cut on uppers, tips on heels, black straw bonnet, trimmed black ve[lvet].

I made enquiries and was informed by Mrs Emma Green, a widow, New Cottage adjoining, and Mr Walter Purkis, Essex Wharf, opposite, also of William Cour[t] Night Watchman to Messrs Brown

& Eagle, Bucks Row, and PC 81GER. Police on [duty] at Wharf near, none of whom heard any scream during the night, or anything to lead them to believe that the murder had been committed there.

The stations and premises of the East London and District Railways, al[l] the wharves and enclosures in the vicinity have been searched but no traces of any weapon could be found there.

PC states he passed through Bucks Row at 3.15 am and PS10 Kirby about the same time, but the woman was not there then and is not known to them.

[sgd] J Spratling Insp
J Keating Supt

Annie Siffey alias Chapman

On the night of her murder Annie Chapman had drinking in a nearby pub and when she returned to Crossingham's Lodging House at 35 Dorset Street, the deputy, Timothy Donovan, demanded money for a bed. Not having the money, Donovan told her to leave.

A night watchman, John Evans, saw her leave about 1.45 a.m. going off in the direction of Brushfield Street. He reported that she had been eating baked potatoes and was 'the worse for drink'. There are no known further sightings of her until around the times of her murder.

Chapman was found dead at 5.50 a.m. by John Davis, one of the residents at 29 Hanbury Street. In the absence of Inspector Reid, who was on holiday, the investigation was initially taken up by

Inspector Joseph Chandler:

METROPOLITAN POLICE
H Division
8th September 1888

I beg to report that at 6.10 am 8th inst while on duty in CommercialStreet, Spitalfields, I received information that a woman had been murdered. I at once proceeded to No 29 Hanbury Street, and in the back yard found a woman lying on her back, dead, left arm resting on left breast, legs drawn up, abducted small intestines and flap of the abdomen lying on he right side, above right shoulder attached by a cord with the rest of the intestines inside the body; two flaps of skin from the lower part of the abdomen lying in a large quantity of blood above the left shoulder; throat cut deeply from left and back in jagged manner right around throat. I at once sent for Dr. Phillips Div Surgeon and to the Station for the ambulance and assistance. The doctor pronounced life extinct and stated the woman had been dead at least two hours. The body was then removed on the Police ambulance to the Whitechapel mortuary.

On examining the yard I found on the back wall of the house (at the head of the body) and about 18 inches from the ground about 6 patches of blood varying in size from a sixpenny piece to a point, and on the wooden pailing [sic] on left of the body near the head patches and smears of blood about 14 inches from the ground.

J L Chandler Inspr

Jack the Ripper

Elizabeth Stride

After a lull of nearly two weeks, two more equally brutal murders were committed in the early hours of Sunday, 30 September.

The first body was found at 1 a.m. in Dutfield's Yard, next to the International Working Men's Educational Club at 40 Berner Street. At the entrance to the yard, which was just over 9 feet wide, were two gates, one of them fitted with a wicket gate that was used when the gates were shut. Although after midnight the lights from the club were still streaming out of the first-floor windows.

The steward of the club was Louis Diemschutz, a traveller in cheap costume jewellery. It was 1.00 a.m. when he arrived back at the club and turned his pony and trap into Dutfield's Yard. As he drove in, the horse shied twice to the left and Diemshutz's looked down to what appeared to be a heap of clothes on the ground. Poking it with his whip he then got down from the trap and realising it was a woman's body, and rushed into the club for help. At the time Diemschutz's discovered the body, well over thirty members of the club were still upstairs singing. PC Henry Lamb and another constable were found patrolling in Commercial Road, and ran to the scene of the murder.

Nearly three weeks after the murder, Chief Inspector Donald Swanson wrote an in-depth report for the Home Office, the first page of which provides further details of the events which followed Lamb's arrival at the scene of the murder:

METROPOLITAN POLICE
Criminal Investigation Department
Scotland Yard
19th day of October, 1888

MURDER IN RETROSPECT

SUBJECT Murder of Elizabeth Stride at Duffields [sic] Yard, Berner Street

Body found at 1am
30th Sept. 1888

I beg to report that the following are the particulars respecting the murder of Elizabeth Stride on the morning of 30th Sept.1888.-

1 am 30th Sept. a body of a woman was found with the throat cut, but not otherwise mutilated by Louis Diemshitz (Secretary to the Socialist Club) inside the gates of Duffield's [sic]Yard in Berner St. Commercial Road East, who gave information to the police. PC 252 Lamb proceeded with them to the spot & sent for Drs. Blackwell & Philips.

1.10 am Body examined by the Doctors mentioned who pronounced life extinct, the position of the body was as follows;- lying on the left side, left arm extended from elbow, cachous lying in hand, right arm over stomach back of hand & inner surface of wrist dotted with blood, legs drawn up knees fixed feet close to wall, body still warm, silk handkerchief round throat, slightly torn corresponding to the angle of right jaw, throat deeply gashed and below right angle apparent abrasion of skin about an inch and a quarter in diameter.

Search was made in the yard but no instrument found.

From enquiries made it was found that at:-
12.35 am 30th PC 452H Smith saw a man and woman the later

with a red rose talking in Berner Street, this P.C. on seeing the body identified it as being that of the woman whom he had seen & he thus describes the man at his age about 28. ht. 5ft. 7in: comp. dark, small dark moustache, dress black diagonal coat, hard felt hat, white collar & tie.

12.45 am 30th Israel Schwartz of 22 Helen Street, Backchurch Lane stated that at that hour on turning into Berner St from Commercial Road & had got as far as the gateway where the murder was committed he saw a man stop & speak to a woman, who was standing in the gateway. The man tried to pull the woman into the street, but he turned her round & threw her down on the footway & the woman screamed three times, but not very loudly. On crossing to the opposite side of the street he saw a second man standing lighting his pipe. The man who threw the woman down called out apparently to the man opposite side of the road "Lipski" & then Schwartz walked away, but finding that he was followed by the second man he ran as far as the railway arch but the man did not follow so far. Schwartz cannot say whether the two men were together or known to each other. Upon being taken to the mortuary Schwartz identified the body as that of the woman he had seen & he thus describes the first man who threw the woman down:- age about 30 ht. 5ft. 5in. comp. fair hair dark, small brown moustache , full face, broad shouldered, dress, dark jacket & trousers black cap with peak, had nothing in his hands.

Second man age 35 ht. 5ft. 11in. comp. fresh, hair light brown, moustache brown, dress dark overcoat, old black hard felt hat wide brim, had a clay pipe in his hand.

(sd) Donald S Swanson

Ch. Insp.

Catherine Beddowes [sic]

Unlike the previous murders, the Catherine Eddowes investigation would be in the hands not of the Metropolitan police, but the City of London police within whose boundaries the murder occurred. Responsible for only one square mile, the City police were answerable to the Corporation of London, whereas Sir Charles Warren, the Commissioner of the Metropolitan Police was answerable to the Home Secretary.

Shortly after the discovery of Elizabeth Stride's body at 1.00 a.m., Catherine Eddowes was released from Bishopsgate Street police station where she had been since 8.45 p.m. the previous evening, having been found drunk on the pavement outside 29 Aldgate High Street. Within forty minutes of her release from Bishopsgate Street police station Catherine Eddowes was dead.

Mitre Square had three entrances, one from Mitre Street and passages from Duke Street and St James's Place. On two sides of the square there were warehouses, belonging to Kearley and Tonge, with a watchman on night duty. On the third side, opposite where the body was found, there were two old houses, one of which was unoccupied and the other lived in by a policeman. On the fourth side were three empty houses. Every fifteen minutes during the night the square was patrolled by a PC 881 Edward Watkins. At 1.30 a.m. the square had been empty when he passed through. At 1.45 a.m. he returned, entering the square from Mitre Street, and saw a woman's body lying on her back on the pavement.

Her throat had been cut, and a host of other mutilations were clear to see. He immediately ran over to the opposite side of the square, to the Kearley and Tonge Warehouse, where he found George Morris, the night watchman inside sweeping up and called for his help. Watkins was no doubt suffering from shock at the sight he had just witnessed as Morris's first thought was that the policemen was unwell. Taking a quick look at the body with his lamp, Morris then ran off to summon help. In nearby Mitre Street he came across PC James Harvey.

The City Police Commissioner, Sir James Fraser, was nearing retirement and had been absent for two months. The Eddowes investigation was therefore carried out under the direction of the Assistant Commissioner, Lt. Col. Sir Henry Smith. One of his senior officers, Inspector James McWilliam, Head of the City of London's Detective Department, sheds more light on events in a report to the Home Office following the discovery of the body:

CITY OF LONDON POLICE.
October 27th 1888
Re East End Murders

I beg to report with reference to the recent murders in Whitechapel that, acting upon stringent orders issued by the Commissioner with a view to preventing if possible a repetition of the murders which had previously been committed in Whitechapel and to keep close observation upon all Prostitutes frequenting public-houses and walking the streets, extra men in plain clothes have been employed by this department since August last to patrol the Eastern portion of the City. On the 30th September at 1.45 am a woman since identified as Catherine Eddowes was found with her throat cut & disemboweled in Mitre Square, Aldgate about 300 yards from the City boundary. The Constable who found the body immediately sent for a surgeon and also to the Police Station at Bishopsgate Street and Inspector Collard was on the spot in a few minutes. Detective Constables Halse, Marriot, Outram who had been searching the passages of houses in the immediate neighbourhood of the spot where the murder was committed (& where the doors are left open all night) on hearing of the murder at 1.55 am at once started off in various directions to look for suspected persons. The officer Halse went in the direction of Whitechapel and passed through Goulstone Street – where part of the deceased's apron was subsequently found at 2.20 am; on returning to the Square he heard that part of an apron stained with blood had been found in Goulstone Street, he then went with D.S. Lawley & D.C. Hunt to Leman Street Station and from thence to Gloustone Street where, the spot at which the apron was found was pointed out to him. On the wall above it was written in chalk "The Jews are the men that will not be blamed for nothing." Halse remained by the writing and Lawley and Hunt returned to Mitre Square.

(sgd) Jas. McWilliam
Inspector

Marie Jeanette Kelly

The terribly mutilated body of Mary Jane Kelly, aged 25, was found lying on her bed in Room 13, Miller's Court, at the rear of 26 Dorset Street. The body was discovered by Thomas Bowyer, an employee of John McCarthy the landlord, who was calling by for the rent.

Very little material is contained in Kelly's victim file, certainly compared to that in the other victim files. So scant is the file, that we have to rely on an interview McCarthy and Bowyer gave to the *Sunday Times* on 10 November, the day after the murder.

According to John McCarthy:

> It is a rule to collect the rent from the Court daily, but as Kelly had been having a hard time of late, I had heard, I didn't press her. 'Go to No 13' I said to Bowyer, meaning Kelly's room, and see if she's going to give me any money. Bowyer went, but when he knocked at the door he couldn't get an answer. Thinking it strange he looked through the keyhole and found the key missing. There are two windows that face the court on the left hand side of the room. One of them was broken when Kelly had her row with the man she said was her husband, and the hole had been stopped with a man's old coat, behind a muslin curtain. Bowyer put his hand through the hole, and drew aside the curtain and the coat. Although the man had been a soldier 20 years, and has seen service in India, he will tell you himself that he nearly fainted at the horrible sight that me his eyes. The woman was lying, a naked, bloody mass upon the bed, and mutilated out of all recognition.'

When Bowyer looked again he saw two pieces of flesh on the bedside table and a pool of blood on the floor. Bowyer then ran off to tell McCarthy and the two of them returned to Miller's Court so that McCarthy could see for himself.

According to McCarthy:

When Bowyer came running in to me all scared and trembling, I went to No 13 and put my head through the broken window. I haven't broken my fast since then; the sight made me sick, and it will be many a year before I forget it.'

Bowyer was then sent off to summon the police from Commercial Street police station. Divisional Inspector Walter Beck and several constables returned immediately with Bowyer to Millar's Court. Having verified Bowyer's story, Beck then sent a telegram to Superintendent Arnold, after which Inspector Abberline arrived and ordered the murder scene to be sealed off. Dr Phillips was summoned at 11.00 a.m. and arrived fifteen minutes later.

The door to Kelly's room was not broken open until 1.30 p.m., when Dr Phillips was the first to enter the room, followed by Inspector Abberline.

Rose Mylett alias Lizzie Davis

At 4.15 a.m. on the morning of Thursday 20 December 1888, PC Robert Goulding discovered the body of Rose Mylett in Clarke's Yard in Poplar. Her throat had not been cut, and in fact there were no signs whatever of a struggle or of any mutilations on the body.

It would seem that to begin with, the police were not even sure the death was the result of murder, taking the view it could be an accidental death. At the inquest, however, the Divisional Surgeon took the view that Mylett had been strangled with a cord. On 11 January 1889, Robert Anderson, Assistant Commissioner CID, submitted a six-page report to Commissioner James Monro about the verdict of the inquest held on 9 January. His frustration is evident from the document's first page:

Mr Munro.

I send herewith supt. Steed's report of the inquest upon Catherine Mylett, and also Messrs Wontner's notification of the verdict of 'Wilful Murder.'

The supt. has come to this office to ask instructions in view of this verdict. I have thought it only fair to him and his officers to tell him plainly that neither the evidence given at the inquest, nor the verdict arrived at, affected the judgment I formed when I personally investigated the case on the 22nd ult, and that I did not intend to take any further action in the matter.

Having regard to the Coroner's strictures upon the action of the Police, it may be well to place the facts on record....

Mr. Brownfield made a P.M: on the morning of the 21st and formed the opinion that the woman had been murdered; but this was not communicated to the Police. The first intimation I had of it was derived from the report of the inquest in the Evening Paper, which I took up after midnight on the 21st on my return from a surprise visit to Whitechapel.

Next morning I brought the matter before you, and by your desire I went to Poplar to investigate the case personally, writing to Mr Bond to meet me there. Mr. Bond, however, was unfortunately out of town for the day.

The statements of the officers who found the body, and especially of PS Golding, who impressed me as being an exceptionally safe and reliable witness, seemed so incompatible with the theory of murder that I brought them to the scene of the death, and finally undertook the distasteful task of going on to the mortuary and examining the body myself.

As the result I came to the conclusion that the death had not been caused by homicidal violence.

RA
11:1:89

Alice McKenzie

At 12.25 am on Wednesday 17 July 1889, PC Walter Andrews discovered the body of Alice McKenzie in Castle Alley, Whitechapel. Her throat had been cut and he blew his whistle, which was heard by Sergeant Badham, who immediately came to his assistance.

Badham's report of the same day takes up the story:

17th July 1889

I beg to report that about 12.48 am 17th inst. I visited PC272H Walter Andrews in Castle Alley, Whitechapel. He being on the Beat No 11 on the 4th Section. I said to him alright, he replied alright Sergeant. I then left him and went to visit another PC on an adjoining beat. I had only got about 50 yards from PC 272H when I heard a whistle blow twice. I rushed to the bottom of the Castle Alley and heard PC 272H say come on quick he ran up the alley, and I followed, and on the pavement closer to two vans on the right side of the footway I saw a woman laying on her right side with her clothes half up her waist exposing her abdomen. I also noticed a quantity of blood under her head on the footway. The PC said here's another murder. I directed the PC not to leave the body or let anyone touch it until the Dr. arrived. The PC said it's quite warm as he touched her. I got the assistance of PC 101H here and PC 423 Allen. The former PC I directed to search the place and sent PC 423 for the Doctor, and Inspr. on duty, and upon his return to make search. Other Constables arrived shortly afterwards, also the Local Inspr. Mr Reid CID. I also hailed a passing cab and acquainted the Superintendent of what had taken place.

E Badham Sergt
Thos.Hawkes Insp.

Trunk of a Female

At 5.15 a.m., on Tuesday 10 September 1889 PC William Pennett discovered the headless and legless torso of a woman near the junction of Backchurch Lane and Pinchin Street in Whitechapel. While the torso had a gash across the abdomen, this appeared to have occurred during the course of dismembering the body and was not considered a deliberate or intended mutilation. The following conclusions, outlined in Chief Inspector Donald Swanson's report which was written later that day are of particular interest:

From the surgeons it was ascertained, firstly that as the trunk was so full of blood, death did not take place by cutting the throat, and the absence of the head prevents them saying that it was from violence to it, (which appears to me most probable as the trunk contains no stabs to cause death). What becomes most apparent is the absence of the attack upon the genitals as in the series of Whitechapel murders beginning in Bucks Row and ending in Millars Court. Certainly, if it be a murder there was time enough for the murderer to cut off the head and limbs there was time to mutilate as in the series mentioned.

Frances Coles

On Friday 13 February 1891, PC Ernest Thompson was on his beat when he discovered the body of prostitute Frances Coles under a railway arch in Swallow Gardens, Whitechapel. That same day, Superintendent Thomas Arnold filed a report, of which the following extract is taken:

13th February, 1891

I beg to report that at about 2.15 am this day PC240H Thompson discovered the body of a female lying in the roadway in Swallow Gardens, Royal Mint Street, Whitechapel, and upon turning on his lantern he saw blood issuing from her throat. He immediately blew his whistle when P/S 101H Hyde and 275H Hinton came to his assistance, and the former went for Dr Oxley of Dock Street who quickly attended and pronounced life extinct. PC 275 went to the Station, and Inspector Flanagan at once proceeded to the spot, and sent for Dr. Phillips Divisional Surgeon, myself, the Chief and Local Inspector and as quickly as men arrived dispatched them to carefully search the neighbourhood and make inquiries of any person who could be found likely to give any information. Dr Phillips attended, examined the body and found two cuts in the throat, sufficient to account for death. The body was not mutilated in any other way. Immediately I arrived I ascertained that telegrams had been sent to surrounding Divisions apprising them of the occurrence and asking that careful inquiries should be made, and proceeded to direct other inquiries at Common Lodging Houses &c. The vicinity of Swallow Gardens was carefully searched, and in a space between a water pipe and some brickwork, about 18 yards from where the body was found Insp Flanagan discovered two shillings wrapped in two pieces of old newspaper apparently "Daily News" upon which however there is no date. There is nothing to connect this money with the murder nor has any instrument or article been found likely to afford a clue. The body was removed to Whitechapel Mortuary and searched but nothing of importance was discovered.

The deceased is known to police of this Division as a Prostitute but at present has not been identified by any person, she is aged about 25, length 5feet, hair and an eye brown, dressed in old dark clothes, and appears of a low class. PC240H Thompson who is a young Constable having only joined on 29th Decr. Last states that as he was passing along Chambers [sic] Street towards Swallow Gardens he heard footsteps apparently those of a man, proceeding in the opposite direction towards Mansell Street, but was not sufficiently close to discern the person. This was just immediately before he found the body and he asserts that when he first saw the deceased there was a movement of one of the eyelids, Be that as it may when the body was found it was quite warm & bleeding. The Constables on the adjoining Beats did not see any person passing about the time he mentioned.

T Arnold Supt

With the death of Frances Coles the Whitechapel murders file officially closes with no conclusion, and no murderer or murderers apprehended or charged. Had the police enquiry been put off the scent in some way? Many conspiracy theorists have claimed over the years that the investigation was derailed by a whole cast of sinister forces ranging from the freemasons to the Royal Family. In reality the course of justice was without doubt perverted, but not by such shadowy powers. The direction of the police investigation and the enormous amount of resources and man-hours devoted to the apprehension of Jack the Ripper was obstructed by something a little more down to earth. A power had certainly been unleashed in 1888 that not only changed the whole climate of the investigation but led directly to the perpetrating of a hoax that would have repercussions for over a century.

CHAPTER 3

HANG LEATHER APRON

London in 1888 was a noisy bustling city of enterprise and activity. The city fictionalised by Charles Dickens was a Dickensian reality for the throngs of squalid poor. Bubblings of social discontent were already simmering away among the spawning working classes, not yet empowered of course with union rights, equality or even the right to peaceful assembly in claim of the right to work, the very right to survive even. People recalled that Commissioner Warren had only the year previously ordered the full use of all available truncheon power to bear down mercilessly on defenceless workers as they assembled in Trafalgar Square on Bloody Sunday, 13 November 1887.

But there was more than just this afoot in the late summer of 1888. News of the brutal murders of prostitutes Emma Smith, Martha Tabram and Mary Ann Nichols was spreading and by 31 August had become front page news. With one stroke of his pen, the *Star's* Ernest Parke had not only linked the three unconnected murders of Smith, Tabram and Nichols to create a series, but had already begun painting a picture of the serial killer responsible for their deaths. Neither were readers spared the gory details on 31 August as Parke's eye catching subheadings spelled out the forensic details of the Nichols murder.

HANG LEATHER APRON

HER THROAT CUT FROM EAR TO EAR

The wound was about two inches wide and blood was flowing profusely. She was immediately conveyed to the Whitechapel mortuary, when it was found that besides the wound in the throat the lower part of the abdomen was completely ripped open and the bowels were protruding. The wound extends nearly to her breast, and must have been effected with a large knife. As the corpse lies in the mortuary, it presents a ghastly sight. The victim seems to be between 35 and 40 years of age, and measures 5ft. 2in. in height. The hands are bruised, and bear evidence of having engaged in

A SEVERE STRUGGLE

The brutality of the murder is beyond conception and beyond description. The throat is cut in two gashes, the instrument having been a sharp one, but used in a most ferocious and reckless way. There is a gash under the left ear, reaching nearly to the centre of the throat. Along half its length, however, it is accompanied by another one which reaches around under the other ear, making a wide and horrible hole, and nearly severing the head from the body.

THE GHASTLINESS OF THIS CUT

however, pales into insignificance alongside the other. No murder was ever more ferociously and more brutally done. The knife, which must have been a large and sharp one, was jobbed into the deceased at the lower part of the abdomen, and then drawn upward, not once but twice. The first cut veered to the right, slitting up the groin, and passing over the left hip, but the second cut went straight upward, along the centre of the body, and, reaching to the breast-bone. Such horrible work could only be the deed of a maniac.

It is probably true to say that single, random acts of violence were regarded by many at the time as almost part and parcel of the expected consequence of living in the East End. Such a commonplace view on the cheapness of human life had for some time been noted and fiercely deplored by the *Star*. However, a series of murders, allegedly at the hand of a single killer was an entirely new and different prospect and one that held out numerous opportunities for a news story that could run and run.

As the writer given responsibility for the story by O'Connor, Parke also appreciated that the 'maniac' he had written about the previous week needed an identity if the story was to be sustained. *Star* hacks Frederick Best and Michael O'Brian had already been put on the streets of Whitechapel by Parke to seek out human interest angles and to pick up quotes and comments from anyone with a story to tell. Best's wife Henrietta was born and brought up in Whitechapel, which gave him a great advantage in being able to use her local knowledge and family connections. The *Star* was one of the few papers who employed this method of news gathering, and it was already beginning to pay off. Having spoken to a number of prostitutes in the area, the *Star* hacks were picking up stories about a sinister prowler by the name of 'Leather Apron' who had apparently been threatening a number of them. Given just a four line mention on 4 September, Parke decided to go big with the Leather Apron story the following day as the result of more detailed interviews carried out in the Whitechapel neighbourhood the previous day and night. Under the headline, 'Leather Apron – The Only Name Linked with Whitechapel Murders', Parke devoted the best part of a page to, 'The Noiseless Midnight Terror' who was attacking Whitchapel's unfortunates:

> He has kicked, injured, bruised and terrified a hundred of them who are ready to testify to the outrages. He has made a certain threat, his favourite threat, to any number of them, and each of the three dead bodies represents that threat carried out. He carries a razor-like knife, and two weeks ago drew it on a woman called 'Widow Annie' as she was crossing the square near London Hospital, threatening at the same time, with his ugly grin and malignant eyes to 'rip her up.'

The feedback and response in terms of paper sales had undoubtedly struck the right chord, as Parke decided to go even bigger with the Leather Apron story the following day, 6 September, devoting further columns to the nameless fiend now described by Parke as, 'Unquestionably Mad.'

> The sense of fear which the murder of the unfortunate woman Nicholls has thrown over the neighbourhood, and especially over her companions, shows no sign of decreasing. A number of the street wanderers are in nightly terror of "Leather-Apron."

> One of our reporters visited one of the single women's lodging-houses last night. It is in Thrawl-street, one of the darkest and most terrible-looking spots in Whitechapel. The house keeps

open till one o'clock in the morning, and reopens again at five. In the house nightly are 66 women, who get their bed for 4d. The proprietor of the place, who is also owner of several other houses of a similar character in the neighbourhood, told some gruesome stories of the man who has now come to be regarded as the terror of the East-end. Night after night, he said, had women come in a fainting condition after being knocked about by "Leather-Apron." He himself would never be out in the neighbourhood after twelve o'clock at night except with a loaded revolver. The "terror," he said, would go to a public-house or coffee-room, and peep in through the window to see if a particular woman was there. He would then vanish, lying in wait for his victim at some convenient corner, hidden from the view of everybody.

The police are making efforts to arrest him, but he constantly changes his quarters. Some of the unfortunate women state that he is now in one of the low slums in the Borough. One of them said she saw him crossing London-bridge as stealthily as usual, with head bent, his skimpy coat turned up about his ears, and looking as if he were in a desperate hurry.

The hunt for "Leather Apron" began in earnest last evening. Constables 43 and 173, J Division, into whose hands "Leather-Apron" fell on Sunday afternoon, were detailed to accompany Detective Ewright, of the J Division, in a search through all the quarters where the crazy Jew was likely to be. They began at half-past ten in Church-street, in Shoreditch, rumour having located the suspected man there. They went through lodging-houses, into "pubs," down side streets, threw their bull's-eyes into every shadow, and searched the quarter thoroughly, but without result.

HANG LEATHER APRON

THE HUNT CONTINUED

later down in the Brick-lane neighbourhood, Florendene-lane being "Leather Apron's" preferred lodging place lately. He was not found here, however, and the search, which then took the direction of the London Hospital, resulted in nothing. It is the general belief that the man has left the district.

The clue furnished by the woman who denounced the man on Sunday is a very unfortunate one. Her offer to prove by two women that "Leather Apron" was seen walking with the murdered woman in Baker's-row at two o'clock last Friday morning, is the most direct bit of evidence that yet has appeared. The belief in "Leather Apron's" guilt, whether it be well or ill founded, is general, and the instant he is recognised by any one he is sure to be reported and arrested. His conduct on Sunday was as usual. He never answers a question when it is put to him, and only speaks under strong compulsion. Mike, the grocer in George's-yard, dwelt a long time last evening on this peculiarity. He knows "Leather Apron" very well, and has known him for six years. He says that

THE MAN IS UNQUESTIONABLY MAD,

and that anybody who met him face to face would know it. That his eyes are never still, but are always shifting uneasily, and he never looks anybody in the eye. "Leather Apron" used to live in the lodging-house around the corner from the grocery, and was turned out of there some months ago with an order not to return. The lodging-house is a few doors below the "model" doorway in which the Turner woman was found with 39 stabs.

Jack the Ripper

After two successive days of Leather Apron features, Parke was clearly running short on inspiration; with little additional street gossip coming in from Best and O'Brian, the Friday 7 September edition of the *Star* carried no more than a reader's letter on the Whitechapel murders. However, any worries about the contents of the Saturday edition were dramatically allayed by the gruesome discovery of the badly mutilated body of Annie Chapman, found at 6.00 a.m. on the morning of Saturday 8 September in the back yard of 29 Hanbury Street. Under the front page headline 'Horror Upon Horror', Parke worked quickly to get the story out in the *Star's* first edition of the day:

> London lies to-day under the spell of a great terror. A nameless reprobate - half beast, half man - is at large, who is daily gratifying his murderous instincts on the most miserable and defenceless classes of the community. There can be no shadow of a doubt now that our original theory was correct, and that the Whitechapel murderer, who has now four, if not five, victims to his knife, is one man, and that man a murderous maniac. There is another Williams in our midst. Hideous malice, deadly cunning, insatiable thirst for blood - all these are the marks of the mad homicide. The ghoul-like creature who stalks through the streets of London, stalking down his victim like a Pawnee Indian, is simply drunk with blood, and he will have more. The question is, what are the people of London to do? Whitechapel is garrisoned with police and stocked with plain-clothes men. Nothing comes of it. The police have not even a clue. They are in despair at their utter failure to get so much as a scent of the criminal.
>
> The unfortunates who are the objects of the man-monster's

malignity should be shadowed by one or two of the amateur patrols. They should be cautioned to walk in couples. Whistles and a signalling system should be provided, and means of summoning a rescue force should be at hand. We are not sure that every London district should not make some effort of the kind, for the murderer may choose a fresh quarter now that Whitechapel is being made too hot to hold him.

We do not think that the police will put any obstacle in the way of this volunteer assistance. They will probably be only too glad to have their efforts supplemented by the spontaneous action of the inhabitants. But in any case, London must rouse itself. No woman is safe while this ghoul is abroad. Up, citizens, then, and do your own police work!

Rumours were reported in the *Pall Mall Gazette* on the same day that a leather apron was found near the scene of the blood stained spot where Annie Chapman's body had been found. There could be no doubt, it was determined in the same report that such property belonged to a local man named none other than Leather Apron. As much as Parke would have loved to exploit this find, he knew full well that the apron belonged to one John Richardson, whose mother lived at 29 Hanbury Street. Richardson had been interviewed at the scene by either Best or O'Brian and as a result Parke knew that the apron was ruled out as evidence by the police before going to press. All was not lost, though as this knowledge enabled him to brickbat the *Gazette*, the *Star's* main radical rival for peddling an inaccurate story.

In their editions of 8 September, both papers were also harshly critical of Chief Commissioner Warren and the police force for their gross ineptitude and lack of street knowledge. The *Star* even urged the citizens of Whitechapel to form vigilante committees to patrol their own districts since Warren clearly knew so little about conditions there. How was it, wondered the *Gazette*, that the police could have the certain resolve to manhandle thousands of workers against the right of free assembly in Trafalgar Square only a year ago and yet seem powerless or incapable of rooting out a single, savage killer of a few, wretched women? Could Scotland Yard even be trusted, asked the *Star*, to handle even the most ordinary of crimes? Serious doubts were been raised in the minds of the ordinary public. Just how confident, or not could they be in their police force?

What was certain by now was that all of Fleet Street recognised a major murder mystery story and in the four days between 10 to 14 September, the leading papers devoted three times more column inches to reporting the Chapman murder than they had with Mary Ann Nichols. With nine sessions of the Chapman and Nichols inquests spread out over most of September, Fleet Street was well able to keep the story of mutilation and murder alive for the rest of the month in among many other false lead stories and wild conjectures about the killer's identity and motives.

As the weeks went by, the accusations of bungling by Scotland Yard mounted and even a few radical newspapers found themselves crying out for more police patrols to alleviate the fears of east-enders about predators in their midst. In the *Star's* 10 September edition Parke once again urged east-enders to form vigilance committees to counter the ineffectiveness of police and detectives.

It was on the morning of 10 September that O'Connor and Parke had news of Leather Apron's arrest, which was announced in the fifth edition of that day's paper:

HANG LEATHER APRON

About nine o'clock this morning a detective arrested a man as "Leather Apron," who was wanted in connection with the Whitechapel murder, at 22, Mulberry-street, Commercial-street. The real name of the man arrested is John Piser, but his friends deny that he has ever been known under the nickname of "Leather Apron." When the detective called at the house the door was opened by Piser himself.

"JUST THE MAN I WANT,"

said the detective, who charged him on suspicion of being connected with the murder of the woman Sivvy. The detective searched the house, and took away some finishing tools which Piser is in the habit of using in his work. By trade he is a boot finisher, and for some time has been living at Mulberry-street with his stepmother (Mrs. Piser) and a married brother, who works as a cabinet-maker. When he was arrested by the detective this morning his brother was at work, and the only inmates of the house were the prisoner's stepmother, his sister-in-law, and a Mr. Nathan, for whom he has worked. His mother and his sister-in-law declared positively to a representative of the Press Association that Piser came home at half-past ten on Thursday night, and

HAS NOT LEFT THE HOUSE SINCE

Our reporter writes: - The man arrested by Detective-Sergeant Thick is now at Leman-street Station. He fits the description of "Leather Apron" exactly, and this similarity is the cause of his arrest. He denies, however, that he is the man wanted, and says he never wore a leather apron in the streets. He is waiting, however, to be recognised, or the contrary, by some people from Wilmot's Lodging House who know "Leather Apron" well. He went along submissively with Detective-Sergeant Thick. His stepmother and his stepsister deny in the strongest terms that he is "Leather Apron."

Any euphoria on Parke's part concerning the column inches that could now be devoted to the Piser story was short lived, as much to the amazement of local residents and press alike, Piser was released, and Parke had to write a very different story to the one he was anticipating in the *Star's* 12 September edition:

John Piser was released last evening at eight o'clock, and was received by his friends and neighbours in Mulberry-street, with enthusiastic shouts of welcome. Some East-end Liberals to whom it now appears he is well known, and among whom he has been an active worker, have also called to sympathise with the family in the trouble apparently brought upon them by a police blunder, and also to congratulate John Piser on his release with unstained character. The detectives searched with unusual diligence, but could find positively nothing against him. And this is not surprising considering that he is not "Leather Apron," at least not the "Leather Apron" who has been the terror and blackmailer of the women of Whitechapel. John Piser, as the suspected "Leather Apron," was kept at Leman-street Police Station for 36 hours, but so far as we can learn he does not seem to have been done the justice of being confronted with any of the women who describe a man named "Leather Apron" as their terror, and who could immediately have put John Piser's identity to a conclusive test. We shall probably have some more to say about this.

HANG LEATHER APRON

Bearing in mind the campaign the *Star* had waged against Piser, it is hardly surprising that he declined to be interviewed by the paper on his release. Instead, O'Connor had to do something he very rarely did, rely on a news agency. In this case, it would appear he had very little choice. The alternative was to go to press with no Piser interview at all. Therefore, on 11 September the *Star* ran the following:

> A Press Association reporter interviewed Piser at 22, Mulberry-street, Whitechapel, this morning. He was released from Leman-street at half-past eight o'clock last evening. The ex-prisoner, in reply to questions put to him, said: - "Whatever particulars the world at large, the police authorities, and the public wish to know as to my whereabouts, and as to where I was staying when these atrocious and horrible crimes were committed I am quite willing to give. I came into this house at a quarter to eleven o'clock on Thursday night last. I knocked at the door. My sister opened it. She was rather surprised to see me, but it is usual at Jewish holiday times to pay visits to friends. My sister's young man was present. I shook hands with him. We had some conversation about work. My sister first went to bed and put the bolt in the latch. Anybody that goes out of the house after the door is latched cannot get in again. From Thursday night until I was arrested
>
> I NEVER LEFT THE HOUSE
>
> except to go into the yard. I was several times seen going into the yard by a next door neighbour. On Monday morning last Sergeant Thick came here. I opened the door. He said I was wanted, and I asked what for. He replied, 'You know what for. You will have to

come with me.' I said, 'Very well, sir. I'll go down to the station with you with the greatest of pleasure.'" "Did he charge you?" asked the reporter, "or tell you what you were wanted for?" He said, "You know you are 'Leather Apron,' or words to that effect. Up to that moment I did not know that I was called by that name. I have been in the habit of wearing an apron. I have worn it coming from my employment, but not recently. I was quite surprised when Sergeant Thick called.

Ominously for the *Star*, Piser alluded in the Press Association interview to the treatment he had received at their hands:

The Star has published a portrait intended to represent me, but it has no more resemblance to me than it has to the man in the moon. I have been told that I shall be wanted at the inquest this afternoon.

At the inquest later that day, Piser gave an account of himself and his recent movements, and explained that he had been in virtual hiding, running the risk of being lynched by angry mobs convinced that he was the murderer:

John Piser: I am a shoemaker and reside at 22 Mulberry Street, Commercial Road. I go by the nickname of 'Leather Apron'. On Thursday night last I arrived home at a quarter before eleven o'clock. My brother, sister and stepmother live there. I remained indoors there until I was arrested by a sergeant of police on Monday last. I had never left the house from the time I entered it until I was apprehended.

Coroner: Why did you remain indoors?

Piser: Because my brother advised me to do so.

Coroner: You were the subject of suspicion were you not?

Piser: I was the subject of false suspicion.

Coroner: You stayed in on the advice of your friends. That was not the best advice that could be given you.

Piser: I will tell you the reason why. I should have been torn to pieces.

Coroner: I have called you partly in your own interest in order to give you the opportunity of clearing your name. Where were you on Thursday, the 30 August?

Piser: On Thursday, the 30 of August and the Friday, I was staying in a common lodging house in Holloway Road. I slept there for the night. I went into the lodging house about 2.15 on Friday morning and went out at eleven that morning. I went out as far as the Seven Sisters Road and on returning saw the reflection of a fire. It was then about half past one, to the best of my recollection. I went as far as the Highbury railway station on the same side of the way and returned back and went into the lodging house. I paid in fourpence and sat for a while on the form in the kitchen smoking a pipe and then went to bed, and got up at eleven o'clock.

Coroner: Did they turn you out?

Piser: The day man came up and told us to get up as he wanted to make the beds. I got up at once, dressed and went down into the kitchen.

Coroner: I think it is only fair to say that the statements of the witness have been corroborated.

Foreman: I think the jury are of the opinion that he is cleared.

Piser: Sergeant Thick, who arrested me has known me for eighteen years.

Coroner: Well, well. I do not think it is necessary for you to say any more.

Jack the Ripper

Understandably he felt aggrieved at the way the *Star* had treated him. They had sold a good few papers at his expense and were now behaving as if the whole saga had been a good natured error. The *Star* might well have felt that they had drawn a line under the episode, but had they really heard the last of Mr Piser?

CHAPTER 4

DEAR BOSS

Rather like a crude barometer of public interest in the Whitechapel murders, O'Connor saw the paper's circulation figures as guiding the direction and nature of the *Star's* coverage.

The *Star's* trail-blazing emphasis on the single killer pitch had seen its circulation rocket from an average of 143,000 copies sold per day before the murders began, to an average daily sale of 232,000 by the time of the Annie Chapman murder on 8 September. This massive jump of sixty two per cent in sales meant that for the first time the *Star's* boastful masthead was actually true – thanks to the Whitechapel murders, O'Connor's fictional claim had become fact - the *Star* now had, without any shadow of a doubt, the 'Largest circulation of any evening paper in the Kingdom'.

Sales were further accelerated by Ernest Parke's intuitive instinct to demonise Leather Apron and run with the story for all it was worth. By the time of Leather Apron's arrest on the morning of 10 September, the *Star's* average daily circulation had leapt a further 13 per cent to reach the giddy heights of 261,100! When, much to Parke's shock and surprise, Piser was released at 9.30 p.m. the following day, the circulation balloon burst and sales fell back to 190,033. With the spectre of Leather Apron now gone, it was clear that Piser had sold his last newspaper.

To compound Parke's troubles, on 13 September, the day after he had testified at the Chapman Inquest, Piser came knocking on the door of the *Star* Building in Stonecutter Street, bold as brass and full of righteous pique. He demanded to see the editor but O'Connor was conveniently out of the office attending parliament. With Massingham, the assistant editor, indignantly declaring that Piser was not his problem, it was left to Parke to defuse the angry visitor.

Parke had committed to print a host of statements that were tantamount to declaring Piser guilty of three murders. Nine days earlier, for example, he had told *Star* readers that, 'he is a more ghoulish and devilish brute than can be found in all the pages of shocking fiction.' Such was the frenzy whipped up by the paper that Piser had been unable to walk the streets for fear of being lynched.

O'Connor later paid tribute to Parke's 'extraordinary shrewdness', in dealing with Piser. While falsely claiming in his memoirs that Piser was invited to the *Star* office as opposed to turning up of his own account, O'Connor conceded that:

The poor man was quite innocent, and we had given him an opportunity of an action with thumping damages. Parke parried this blow by inviting 'Leather Apron' to come and see him at the office. 'Leather Apron' made a demand for a hundred pounds for his assent to abandon all legal proceedings. Parke insisted on fifty pounds. When the man still dissented, Parke made the counter proposition that he would tell 'Leather Apron' where to get another fifty pounds which would make up the hundred pounds he claimed. 'Leather Apron' assented; and Parke then revealed to him the fact that another paper had made insinuations against him as direct as those of the Star, and that he certainly could get fifty pounds from them. The bargain was made, and by this bit of information and by our gift of fifty pounds we were kept out of an action which might have cost us thousands of pounds.

Although Piser was clearly innocent in of any association with the murders, he was perhaps lucky in retrospect to have walked away with the money he did. Had the case ever gone before a libel jury it might well have come out that only the previous month, on 4 August, he had been charged with indecent assault. Although the case had been dismissed on account of his female accuser failing to appear in court, this episode might indicate that so far as the intimidation complaints the *Star* had highlighted were concerned, it might well have been a case of no smoke without fire.

Despite Parke's adept handling of Piser, the paper's proprietors soon got wind of the close shave they, and their coffers had just had and berated O'Connor for his cavalier recklessness. It is worth bearing in mind that O'Connor's claim, written some forty years after the event, that the sum expended was £50, was never corroborated by Parke, who along with Massingham was known to have viewed O'Connor's memoirs with some disdain. Anecdotal rumour in 1888 was very much to the effect that the sum the *Star* had to part company with was at least £500 if not more. While it is unlikely that we will ever know for sure, a higher sum might help explain the swift rebuke of the proprietors. Not for the first time would Brunner or Colman harp on about journalistic ethics while at the same time expecting high and sustained sales.

With potential litigation gone, Parke was now on the look-out for another Leather Apron, a ghoulish suspect who could again ignite paper sales in the dramatic and immediate way Piser had done.

Jack the Ripper

This time round he knew he had to be wary; any more slip-ups like the one from which he had just extricated the paper would certainly lead to crippling damages for the infant paper and the dismissal of all concerned by Brunner and Colman.

To O'Connor too, the settling of the Piser episode brought mixed emotions; relief that the threat of damages had finally been lifted, but gloom and despondency in equal measure that the milchcow that had made him the toast of Fleet Street had vanished as quickly as it appeared.

To cap it all, a further missive from Colman was received berating the paper's 'vulgar tone'. Never one to hold back in defending himself, O'Connor shot off an immediate riposte pointing out that, Londoners had to be, 'stirred-up', and that 'mild arguments' about reform would not do.

O'Connor's frustration is evident from his editorial written the day after Piser's visit and the very day of Colman's missive:

> There will be a perceptible tightening of public interest in the Whitechapel tragedies to-day. Nearly a week has passed since the final crime in the series, and still the police are at fault. Meanwhile, the epidemic of lawlessness continues. Three violent robberies have taken place within a hundred yards of each other, and midway between the scenes of the last two crimes. There has been one more mysterious crime in the West of London, to which the police have no clue. The evidence at the inquest is bad – bad as can be. Mysterious personages flit through it like the shadowy and awful figures in POE and STEVENSON'S novels, or the stealthy and cunning assassins of GABORIAU and DU BOISGOBEY. The body of woman is washed at the mortuary – nobody knows by whom. A ghostly

pensioner starts into view and disappears again. Every new turn of this bewildering labyrinth reveals some fresh depth of social blackness, some strange and repulsive curiosity of human nature. What are we to do? Where are we to turn?

Within two weeks of O'Connor's melancholy editorial an answer to his prayers appeared from the 'bewildering labyrinth'. Far exceeding the macabre imaginations of Poe and Stevenson, this new Whitechapel ghoul would announce his arrival literally on O'Connor's doorstep.

Number 5 New Bridge Street was two minutes walk from the *Star's* Stonecutter Street office and was home to the Central News Agency, run by one John Moore. During the previous decade, a number of news agencies had come into existence to answer the increasing call for made-to-measure news that could be syndicated to the growing number of papers, particularly in the provinces. Partisan politics also played its hand in the news agency business. For example, of the two leading outfits, Moore's Central News was seen as Conservative aligned while the National Press Agency leant in the opposite direction. Indeed, a decade before, O'Connor had been dismissed by Central News, where his very brief tenure in the reporter's gallery at the House of Commons was cut short due to a personality clash with the editor. Despite the passage of time, the dismissal was apparently something that still rankled with O'Connor, who rarely missed an opportunity for a dig at the agency's expense.

Adding to his vexation in late September was the Unionist reaction to the Parnell Commission. Set up by an Act of Parliament to investigate various claims made by *The Times* in March 1887 against Charles Stewart Parnell, the Commission's investigations were a continual source of news throughout 1888 and the following year. The principal allegation was contained in a facsimile letter, allegedly bearing his signature, which condoned the 1882 murder of the Permanent Under-Secretary for Ireland, T.H. Burke. Although Parnell immediately declared it a forgery, the Tory press and their allied news sources, such as Central News, had a field day with the accusations.

On 28 September 1888, Central News would themselves become the recipients of a letter that was destined to make an even more dramatic impact than the Parnell letter, although few appreciated its notoriety at the time of receipt. This letter, purporting to have been written by the Whitechapel murderer, has subsequently come to be known as the 'Dear Boss' letter. The police and the public believed that in these lines they were actually hearing the voice of the killer ...

25. Sept. 1888.

Dear Boss

I keep on hearing the police have caught me but they wont fix me just yet. I have laughed when they look so clever and talk about being on the right track. That joke about Leather Apron gave me real fits. I am down on Whores and I shant quit ripping them till I do get buckled. Grand work the last job was. I gave the lady no time to squeal. How can they catch me now. I love my work and want to start again. You will soon hear of me with my funny little games. I saved some of the proper <u>red</u> stuff in a ginger beer bottle over the last job to write with but it went thick and like glue and I cant use it. Red ink is fit enough <u>ha. ha.</u> The next job I do I shall clip the lady s ears off and send to the police officers just for jolly wouldnt you. Keep this letter back till I do a bit more work then give it out straight. My knife's so nice and sharp I want to get to work right away if I get a chance. Good Luck.

Yours truly
Jack the Ripper

Don't mind me giving the trade name

A hurried post-script was added at the foot of the letter:

wasn't good enough to post this before I got all the red ink off my hands curse it.
No luck yet. They say I'm a doctor now <u>ha ha</u>

Although dated 25 September, the letter was not actually posted until the 27 September. Following its arrival at Central News later the same day (the Victorian postal service was in many ways superior to our own), a debate apparently took place as to whether it was genuine or not. Eventually, on Moore's authority, it was forwarded to Chief Constable Adolphus Williamson on Saturday 29 by Central News journalist Thomas Bulling with a covering note:

The editor presents his compliments to Mr Williamson & begs to inform him the enclosed was sent to the Central News two days ago, & was treated as a joke.

This was the first time the name Jack the Ripper had ever been used and as soon as the letter was made public knowledge it was to cause a massive sensation. The name Jack the Ripper was a journalist's dream. Now, suddenly, the Whitechapel murderer had a name and with it a sense of personality. He was no longer just a generic 'fiend' or 'devil' he was Jack the Ripper. By writing the letter the killer appeared to be both taunting the police and showing that he relished the publicity.

As with so many other aspects of the investigation, police opinion about the authenticity of the 'Dear Boss' letter seems to be divided. Sir Charles Warren made his views clear two weeks later in a letter to Godfrey Lushington, the Permanent Under-Secretary of State at the Home Office:

> Thanks for memo of Mr Troop. We will look into the matter at once. It is rather a difficult matter. I do not know whether the P.O. can tell in what letter boxes the letter of Jack the ripper is posted. At present I think the whole thing is a hoax but of course we are bound to try & ascertain the writer in any case.

Equally, it seems clear that as late as 1896 Chief Inspector Henry Moore at Scotland Yard (who had assisted Inspector Abberline at the time of the murders and taken over from him in March 1889) was using the 'Dear Boss' letter to gauge the authenticity of subsequent crank letters that were sent or referred to the police.

However, at the time of receipt, there had been little opportunity for pondering on the 'Dear Boss' letter's authenticity, for within twenty-four hours, events had taken a further dramatic turn. In the early hours of Sunday 30 September, the murders of Elizabeth Stride and Catherine Eddowes took place. Eddowes' mutilations seemed to confirm that this letter could possibly be genuine, for in it the author had written, 'the next job I do I shall clip the lady's ears off and send to the police officers just for jolly', and Eddowes' earlobe appeared to have been cut off. It is widely disputed whether this was intentional or incidental as she had so many injuries to her face. The killer certainly didn't keep the earlobe or post it to the police as promised because it was found at the crime scene. Nevertheless, the injury to the ear meant that this letter was now taken a whole lot more seriously by the police than it had been the day before.

The 'Dear Boss' letter was quickly followed by the equally notorious 'Saucy Jacky' postcard which arrived at the Central News Agency on Monday 1 October:

> I wasn't codding dear old Boss when I gave you the tip, you'll hear about saucy Jackys work tomorrow double event this time number one squealed a bit couldn't finish strait off. had not time to get ears for police thanks for keeping last letter back till I got to work again
>
> Jack the Ripper

For many subsequent Ripper writers who assumed the postcard had been posted on the Sunday, this message was a clincher in terms of authenticity. Only the murderer, they argued, would have known the details of the 'double-event', which were not published in the press until the following day, Monday 1 October. Also, only the murderer could have known that Stride had 'squealed a bit' … ('but not very loudly' according to witness Israel Schwartz) and apparently, as a consequence, had not the time to cut off her ears.

However, their assumption that it had been posted on 30 September was in fact wrong, something almost certainly picked up on by Scotland Yard, who must surely have noted that the card bore the postmark of 1 October. As previously remarked upon, same day postal collections and deliveries were not uncommon in Victorian London. In fact, the first collection on Monday morning was 3.00 a.m.

On 1 October two newspapers, the *Evening News* and the *Star*, broke the story about the Ripper letter and postcard being received by Central News. The *Evening News* was one of Central News's biggest customers. Founded in 1881 by Coleridge Kennedy and Harry Marks, it initially took a Liberal tone, but within a year it had been sold to the Conservative Newspaper Company Ltd. The new proprietors not unnaturally closely aligned their new paper to the agency that was often referred to as 'the mouthpiece of the Conservative Party' ... Central News. A cursory read of the *Evening News* in 1888, for example, was notable for the number of stories attributed to Central News or Central News reporters.

It was not surprising then that they were the first to be given this exclusive by John Moore. This is testified to at the very beginning of the *Evening News* article, which appeared in the paper's fifth edition:

> Central News gives us the following information, namely, that on Thursday last a letter bearing the EC post mark, directed in red ink, was delivered at their agency.

Unbeknown to *Evening News* readers, what followed was a version of the letter that was noteworthy for the fact that in several respects it differed somewhat from the original letter. The version printed by the *Evening News* (with all the missing punctuation marks missing from the original now inserted) is reproduced below with the differences to the original text in italics:

DEAR BOSS

September 25, 1888

Dear Boss – I keep on hearing the police have caught me, but they won't fix me just yet. I have laughed when they look so clever and talk about being on the right track. That joke about Leather Apron gave me *rare* fits. I am down on whores, and I shan't quite ripping them till I do get buckled. Grand work the last job was. I gave the lady no time to squeal. How can they catch me now. I love my work. I want to start again. You will soon hear of me with my funny little games. I saved some of the proper *red* stuff in a ginger beer bottle over the last job. *I did* write with *it* but it went thick like glue, and I can't use it. Red ink is fit enough, (*I hope*) ha ha *ha*. The next job I do I shall clip the lady's ears and send *them* to the police-officers just for *folly*. *Wouldn't you keep* this letter back till I do a bit more work; then give it out *straight?* My knife *is so* nice and sharp, I want to get to work right away if I get a chance. *Good, cock,*

Yours truly,
JACK THE RIPPER.

Don't mind me giving the trade name. Wasn't good enough to post this before I got all the red ink off my hands curse it. No luck yet. They say I'm a doctor *now. Ha! ha! ha! ha! ha!*

Why this alternative version of the letter should be released to the *Evening News* is somewhat puzzling. Because the handwriting of the original was so clear and unambiguous, journalistic misreading of the text is not really a possibility. However, the biggest mystery so far as the reporting of the 'Dear Boss' letter and postcard is

concerned centres not on the role of the *Evening News* but on the
Star.

The *Star* prided itself on procuring its stories from first hand
sources, and as we have previously noted, had a second to none
team of ferrets who scoured the streets for copy. The majority of
papers at the time, irrespective of political stance, were content to
have journalists spending most of their time in the office gleaning
material from second hand sources, such as news agencies. This
was not only seen by O'Connor as 'lazy journalism' but a hallmark
of the 'old journalism' he so contemptuously sought to replace.

If the *Star* ever published stories that were not provided by its
own journalists, and that was hardly ever, then it was to the Press
Association or the National Press Agency that it resorted. The *Star*
never, as a matter of principle, took Central News copy. If Central
News was ever mentioned in the *Star*, it was on the end of a piece
of invective, such as 'False Reports', on 19 October, revealing that
the Central News story about the city police arresting an American
suspect was completely untrue.

How then was the *Star* in a position to break the story at the same
time as the *Evening News*, bearing in mind it was not a Central
News client and on principle did not touch Central News stories?
Did they have a tip off or indeed another source for the story,
or was there an even more intriguing explanation? The mystery
deepens still further with the discovery that the *Star* actually
appears to have had the story out marginally ahead of the *Evening
News*. Although at first glance it would appear that the 'Dear Boss'
story appeared for the first time in the fifth edition of both papers,
in other words in the early part of the afternoon of 1 October,
this scenario may not in fact be correct. From contemporary *Star*
records, it would seem that another of O'Connor's wheezes was

to call the first edition of the *Star* the second edition. In this way it would appear that his second edition was already on the street, ahead of the game, by the time most papers had their first edition out, and that subsequent editions maintained this momentum. Most evening papers of this era aimed the have their first edition out by mid morning. It would therefore seem that the *Star*'s 'Dear Boss' story was, in reality, in O'Connor's 'fourth' edition, one edition ahead of the *Evening News*.

From another contemporary record, the diary of Mrs Elizabeth O'Connor, we know that her husband was away in Scotland on a speaking engagement at the time of the double murder and the subsequent breaking of the 'Dear Boss' story on the Monday. That day's edition was therefore directed by Assistant Editor Henry Massingham, although O'Connor remained in touch with Stonecutter street by telegram and telephone.

In its coverage that day the *Star* not only broke the Ripper story but managed, at the self same time, to run it as an attack on Central News for again peddling false stories:

A practical joker, who signed himself 'Jack the Ripper', wrote to Central News last week, intimating with labored flippancy that he was going to commence operations again in Whitechapel shortly. He said he would cut the woman's ears off to send to the police. This morning, the same agency received a postcard smeared apparently with dirty blood. It was written with red chalk. It says: -

'I was not codding dear old Boss when I gave you the tip. You'll hear about saucy Jacky's work tomorrow. Double event this time. Number one squealed a bit. Couldn't finish off. Had not time to get ears for police. Thanks for keeping back last letter til I got to work again. – JACK THE RIPPER.'

One unique aspect of the *Star* story, which was never to appear elsewhere, was their claim that the writing on the postcard was done with a red chalk pencil (repeated again in an article on 4 October). Another difference was the perspective they took.

Papers who covered the story in the days to follow, either did so on the basis that the communications could well be from the real killer, or mentioned in passing that a practical joke was not beyond the bounds of possibility. The *Star* was unique in insisting from the start that it was a hoax. Was this simply a unique sixth sense or did they have commercial, political or even legal reasons for adopting this perspective? More mystery about their stance would emerge two days later.

Hoax or no hoax, they certainly had no qualms about exploiting the story to the full. Their fifth edition billboard, used by its newsboys to sell the paper on the street, where the vast majority of copies were sold, simply stated 'JACK THE RIPPER'. While the story itself appeared on the inside pages, it is clear that as with other Ripper stories, these were the ones used as bait by the paper sellers.

The following day, 2 October, a number of Central News provincial client papers such as the *Derby Mercury*, The *East Anglian Daily Times*, and the *Sunderland Post* were offered the story. While expressing the possibility that it could be a practical joke, papers who covered the story, such as the *East Anglian Daily Times*, tended to lean in the same direction as the *Evening News* had done, namely to hedge their bets and if anything to err on the side that it could well be genuine.

This stance, contrary to Thomas Bulling's statement to Adolphus Williamson on 29 September that Central News was 'treating it as a joke', appears to have been the line that Central News was also in fact taking. On 3 October, however, the rug was pulled from under Central News's feet when the Police decided to publish a poster to be displayed by London police stations featuring a facsimile of the 'Dear Boss' Letter and 'Saucy Jacky' postcard. In large bold letters at the foot of the poster it said:

'Any person recognising the handwriting is requested to communicate with the nearest police station'

From this moment on, Central News were unable to market the story as any journalist was now able to walk into his nearest police station and copy down the wording. When the *Daily Telegraph* went one stage further the next day and reproduced an extract of the facsimile copy of the handwriting, the *Star* uniquely came out and attacked them for printing:

facsimiles of the ghastly but very silly letters from 'Jack the Ripper' We were offered them by the Central News and declined to print them. They were clearly written in red pencil, not in blood, the obvious reason being that the writer was one of those foolish but bad people who delight in an unholy notoriety. Now, the murderer is not a man of this kind. His own love of publicity is tempered by a very peculiar and remarkable desire for privacy and by a singular ability to secure what he wants. Nor is there any proof or pre-knowledge of the Mitre Square crimes, beyond the prediction that they were going to happen, which anybody might have had. The reference to ear-clippings may be a curious coincidence, but there is nothing in the posting of the letter on Sunday. Thousands of Londoners had details of the crimes supplied in the Sunday papers.

O'Connor's claim that Central News had offered him a facsimile copy should be treated with extreme scepticism if not downright disbelief. Why would Central News have offered the *Star* or indeed any other newspaper a facsimile copy (presumably at a cost) when such copies were freely available from the police? The claim again allowed O'Connor to take the moral high ground against Central News.

More profoundly, why was the *Star* so against the handwriting being reproduced and seen by hundreds of thousands of readers throughout the country? Had they suddenly become sensitive to the disposition of newspaper readers? It could not be because they were opposed to the actual wording being publicised, as they themselves were the first to print the contents of the 'Saucy Jacky' postcard and would go on to print verbatim, an even more ghoulish letter two weeks later.

Having reached the public at large, a number of readers were now penning missives to editors, remarking on the fact that the letter and postcard contained a number of American phrases that few people in this country were familiar with. In the *Evening News* on 5 October for example, a reader drew attention to, 'boss', 'fix me', 'right track', 'real fits', 'shan't quit', squeal', 'give it out straight', 'right away' and 'fit enough', concluding that, 'many of these expressions are in constant use by all classes of Americans but never by Englishmen'. In fact, *The Daily Telegraph*, following on from their facsimile article made a similar point, speculating that, 'the writer is probably an American or an Englishman who has mixed with our cousins on the other side of the Atlantic.'

A second and more serious repercussion of the wide-spread coverage was that it opened the flood gates to sack-loads of lunatic letters from copycat writers with red ink and active imaginations, which undoubtedly took up vast amounts of valuable police time. Among the deluge was the third (and last) communication from the 'Dear Boss' writer, which arrived at Central News on the morning of 5 October. Again, Thomas Bulling wrote to Chief Constable Adolphus Williamson, but this time with a difference, he merely enclosed the envelope not the actual letter. However, he did reproduce the letter word-for-word within his own:

Dear Mr Williamson

At 5 minutes to 9 o'clock tonight we receive the following letter the envelope of which I enclose by which you will see it is in the same handwriting as the previous communications

5 Oct 1888

Dear Friend

In the name of God hear me I swear I did not kill the female whose body was found at Whitehall. If she was an honest woman I will hunt down and destroy her murderer. If she was a whore God will bless the hand that slew her, for the women of Moab and Midian shall die and their blood shall mingle with the dust.
I never harm any others or the Divine power that protects and helps me in my grand work would quit for ever. Do as I do and the light of glory shall shine upon you. I must get to work

tomorrow treble event this time yes yes three must be ripped. will send you a bit of face by post I promise this dear old Boss. The police now reckon my work a practical joke well well Jacky's a very practical joker ha ha ha Keep this back till three are wiped out and you can show the cold meat.

Yours truly
Jack the Ripper
Yours truly
T J Bulling

We can only speculate as to why Bulling did this. Whatever the reason, it would seem that his or John Moore's decision to do so would have particular consequences for Central News that we shall consider in the next chapter. Suffice to say at this stage that it would seem that the police asked Central News to refrain from disclosing its contents. As a consequence, it did not receive the coverage or publicity the first two communications had done.

The central theme of the letter seems to echo one of the many theories being debated in the press at the time, i.e. the possible motive of religious mania. After an opening reference to the female torso discovered in Whitehall on 2 October, the letter then expands into a religious context, quoting the women of Moab and Midian. According to the Old Testament and the Hebrew Torah, the Israelites, after spending a period of time in the plain of Moab, begin to involve themselves with Moabite prostitutes. A plague which kills 24,000 then follows. When an Israelite Zimri brings a Moabite prostitute into the camp in the sight of Moses, Phinehas, a grandson of Aaron takes a spear and slaughters both Zimri and the prostitute. As a result, the plague immediately ceases.

Despite the moratorium on the third letter or perhaps because of it, Central News decided to issue a story which linked the author of the three communications to the writing found in Goulston Street after the murder of Catherine Eddowes. An extract from the story read as follows:

> The witnesses who saw the writing, however, state that it was similar in character to the letters sent to the Central News and signed 'Jack the Ripper,' and though it would have been far better to have clearly demonstrated this by photography, there is now every reason to believe that the writer of the letter and postcard sent to the Central News (facsimiles of which are now to be seen outside every police station) is the actual murderer. The police, consequently, are very anxious that any citizen who can identify the handwriting should without delay communicate with the authorities.

This hardening of Central News's line about the authenticity of the 'Dear Boss' author to the extent that he was now proclaimed by them to be, 'the actual murderer', was rounded upon by the *Star* on 8 October under the headline 'Revival of Discredited Rumour'. It is also significant that the police themselves rebuked the Central News story in a report from Chief Inspector Donald Swanson to the Home Office on 6 November 1888:

> to those police officers who saw the chalk writing, the handwriting of the now notorious letters to the newspaper agency bears no resemblance at all.

Jack the Ripper

Resemblance or not, one thing was for sure, the Jack the Ripper name was now firmly established, and for various reasons would become retrospectively so. For example, in 1938 former Chief Inspector Walter Dew, who had made his name as the man who had arrested Crippen, published his memoirs. A Detective Constable at the time of the Whitechapel murders, Dew wrote the following about the events of 9 September 1888, the day after the murder of Annie Chapman:

> The whole area was in a panic after they found Annie Chapman's body. The day after the murder I was in Hanbury Street taking statements from people when I saw a man called 'Squibby' standing in the crowd. I knew he was wanted. I also knew that every time he was arrested it took half a dozen policemen to bring him in, and usually by the time they had got him to the station he hadn't got a rag of clothing left on his back, and half the police weren't fit for duty for a while again.

> I was standing with another detective called Stacey when I saw Squibby. But the moment I saw him, he saw me. He dashed across the road and ran off down Commercial Street. Stacey and I went after him drawing our truncheons - plain clothes men carried truncheons during the Ripper murders. But seeing us dash off the crowd started shouting 'Jack the Ripper! Jack the Ripper!'

> Soon there were hundreds of people yelling out and coming after us. I was passing Fashion Street when a big fellow tried to trip me up but I hit him with my truncheon and he fell into the baker's window. Squibby got into Flower and Dean Street, went into the front door of a house, over a back wall and into the house next

door with Stacey and me after him. Finally we grabbed him as he was getting through a window. We were both done in by now and I thought we were going to be really in for it, trying to take Squibby in. But instead of starting to fight, he was shaking like a leaf. Then I realised why. It wasn't us he was scared of – it was the crowd. They were all round the house by now shouting that the Ripper was in there and for us to bring him out so they could lynch him. Messages had been sent to the stations around and eventually when the crowd died down a bit we went downstairs and found scores of policemen clearing a space in front of the house. When we got Squibby out, the crowd went mad again. They rushed us and tried to break through the cordon and get at Squibby. In the end we put him in a four-wheeler and went on in that, with the police forming a cordon all round it. But that wasn't any good either, and they almost turned the cab over several times.

Finally, an inspector called Babbington said we would be better off on foot. The whole of Commercial Street was filled with a yelling mob by now but the police formed a cordon all the way to Commercial Street station. In the end we managed to fight our way into the station. The doors were shut, but the mob stayed outside for hours trying to get in. Nothing we could shout made any difference to them. Squibby was a changed man after that though. As far as I know he never resisted arrest again.

Whatever else may or may not be true in this account, clearly Dew's references to the mob shouting 'Jack the Ripper, Jack the Ripper' and later surrounding a house in Flower and Dean Street calling for the Ripper to be brought out, are at best genuine memory lapses at worst fabrications. It would be another three weeks before the name Jack the Ripper would be born.

As a result of the perceived 'double-event' and the simultaneous arrival of 'Jack the Ripper', newspaper sales again rocketed, none more so than the *Star's*, whose circulation hit 217,158 on 6 October, a jump of fourteen per cent since the decline in sales occasioned by the release of 'Leather Apron'.

Was this profound change of fortune down to an elaborate and skilful hoax or were these the words of the real killer? Who was the author of three communications directed to Central News and what was their motive for giving birth to Jack the Ripper?

CHAPTER 5

THE HIDDEN HAND

Within several days of the publication of the 'Dear Boss' letter, some in the newspaper industry were beginning to smell a rat. However, the journalist George R. Sims, who wrote for the *Referee*, a Sunday newspaper owned by the Weekly Dispatch, was one of the few who actually voiced his thoughts publicly. On 7 October he told readers of his weekly *Referee* column:

> The fact that the self-postcard-proclaimed assassin sent his imitation blood-besmeared communication to the Central News people opens up a wide field for theory. How many among you, my dear readers, would have hit upon the idea of 'the Central News' as a receptacle for your confidence? You might have sent your joke to the Telegraph, the Times, any morning any evening paper, but I will lay long odds that it would never have occurred to you to communicate with the Press agency which serves the entire Press? It is an idea which might occur to a Press man perhaps; and even then it would probably only occur to someone connected with the editorial department of a newspaper, someone who knew what the Central News was, and the place it filled in the business of news supply. This proceeding on Jack's part betrays an inner knowledge of the newspaper world which is

certainly surprising. Everything therefore points to the fact that the jokist is professionally connected with the Press.

Although the suggestion that the three 'Dear Boss' communications were possibly not genuine had been given voice to by a number of papers in October 1888, they certainly had not suggested or implied who might be behind them if it was not the actual killer. Aside from the possible legal repercussions, no mainstream paper had any interest in doing anything that might question or derail the circulation gravy train that had been set in motion by the arrival of 'Jack the Ripper' and his taunting missives.

It would be another two decades before public reservations were again expressed about the 'Dear Boss' communications. This time the mutterings would not be from Fleet Street but from three retired senior officers at Scotland Yard.

In 1910, the former Assistant Commissioner Sir Robert Anderson published his memoirs, 'The Lighter Side of My Official Life', in which he stated:

> I will only add here that the 'Jack-the-Ripper' letter which is preserved in the Police Museum at Scotland Yard is the creation of an enterprising London journalist ... I am almost tempted to disclose the identity of the pressman who wrote the letter above referred to. But no public benefit would result from such a course and the traditions of my old department would suffer.

When Sir Melville Macnaghten retired in 1913, he wasted little time in rushing to print the following year with his memoirs, 'Days of My Years', in which he made the following comment about the writer of the 'Dear Boss' letter:

I have always thought I could discern the stained forefinger of the journalist, indeed, a year later I had shrewd suspicions as to the actual author! But whoever did pen the gruesome stuff, it is certain to my mind that it was not the mad miscreant who had committed the murders. The name 'Jack the Ripper', however, had got abroad in the land and had 'caught on'; it riveted the attention of the classes as well as the masses.

Having worked closely with Anderson as his deputy before taking over the Assistant Commissioner's post in 1903, it is a strong possibility that Macnaghten's view about the journalist responsible was essentially Anderson's. Neither he nor Anderson elaborate on their statements or disclose when in fact they first came to hold these views. Although Macnaghten refers to having suspicions 'a year later', it is not clear to which year he refers. It could either be 1889, a year after the crimes were assumed to have ended, or 1890, a year after Macnaghten joined the Metropolitan Police. As we will see momentarily, a third retired officer former Chief Inspector John Littlechild expressed similar suspicions around the same time as Macnaghten. The main question then, is whether these are three separate theories or in fact one emanating originally from Anderson.

As we have already noted, Macnaghten was Anderson's deputy and the two worked very closely together. Anderson's background was in Irish republic counter-intelligence. In this former capacity he had worked at the Home Office between 1867 and 1886. In 1883, as the result of a wave of Irish republican terrorism, which included a bomb explosion behind the Home Office, the Special Irish Branch (which would later evolve into the Special Branch) was set up by the Metropolitan Police. Superintendent Adolphus Williamson nominated Chief Inspector John Littlechild to head the new branch. Littlechild had spent five months in Dublin assisting the Irish police following the Phoenix Park murders of the previous year and was rightly considered the best man for the job. Anderson was to be the conduit between the new branch and the Home Secretary. In this capacity he worked hand in glove with Littlechild and the two men apparently got on extremely well together and remained friends after their respective retirements.

When George R. Sims, who clearly retained an interest in the Whitechapel murders and the authorship of the 'Dear Boss' letter in particular, wrote to Littlechild in September 1913 the answer he received was a most revealing one. Our awareness of the reply he received only came to light in 1993 when Stewart Evans, later to co-author *The Lodger*, purchased a collection of letters that had belonged to Sims from antiquarian book dealer Eric Barton. One of these was Littlechild's reply to Sims' letter. It finally put a name to the anonymous pressman suspected of having written the 'Dear Boss' letter:

With regard to the term 'Jack the Ripper' it was generally believed at Scotland Yard that Tom Bullen of the Central News was the originator, but it is more probable Moore, who was his chief, was the inventor. It was a smart piece of journalistic work. No journalist of my time got such privileges from Scotland Yard as Bullen.

Littlechild then goes on to recall:

Poor Bullen occasionally took too much to drink and I fail to see how he could help it knocking about so many hours and seeking favours from so many people to procure copy. One night when Bullen 'had taken a few too many' he got early information of the death of Prince Bismarck and instead of going to the office to report it sent a laconic telegram 'bloody Bismarck is dead'. On this I believe Mr Charles Moore fired him out.

Again, with so many retrospective recollections, errors of memory often occur. There was in fact no one by the name of Tom Bullen or Charles Moore at Central News, although it is reasonable to assume that Littlechild was erroneously recalling Thomas Bulling and John Moore. The impression given of 'Bullen' is of a subordinate journalist working under Moore, 'who was his chief.' However, recently discovered records of the Central News Agency Ltd indicate that Thomas J Bulling, although an experienced journalist, was actually a director and shareholder of the company. Littlechild also mentions that 'Bullen' was fired by Moore for failing to file a report on Bismarck's death, which occurred on 30 July 1898. Records show that subsequent to this date Bulling was still a shareholder and director, and remained so for some time.

Irrespective of the Bullen/Bulling issue, the likelihood is that these three expressions of view about the culpable journalist are from one common source, Anderson. However, like Anderson's other pontification about the Jewish Ripper suspect this theory is also caged in uncertainty. Littlechild's letter to Sims has, since its publication, been represented by many to imply a clear naming of Bulling as the 'Dear Boss' fabricator. In fact, the letter is nowhere near as clear and precise on this point. The key sentence in this regard must surely be, 'but it is probable that Moore, his chief was the inventor'. This again can be read in at least two ways, either that it was Moore not Bulling who was suspected of writing it, or that it was written as a result of Moore's instructions or guidance. Whatever the interpretation, this theory is very much open to debate and doubt.

The first and most obvious point here is that at best Littlechild is simply saying that this was a suspicion of others at Scotland Yard. If there were suspicions about Bulling or Moore, then clearly the reason they were not publicly named by Anderson or Macnaghten and remained mere suspicions was that there was not a single shred of evidence to substantiate them. If there was no evidence, what then led Anderson to possibly take this view?

It may well be as simple as the old theory of blaming the messenger. We should also recall that when Bulling wrote to Chief Constable Williamson with regard to the third communication on 5 October, he merely enclosed the envelope, and instead of supplying the letter wrote it out verbatim in his own hand. Although why he did so is not clear. Did the fact that the third letter, set out in Bulling's own hand, put into the mind of the Scotland Yard reader that he was possibly the author?

If Bulling or Moore were behind the scam, one might rightly think that the last thing they would want to do would be to supply the police with such a convenient comparison. After all, as they well knew, the consequences of being unfrocked were particularly serious ones. Two rare examples of Ripper letter-hoaxers being prosecuted were reported in the national press, namely Maria Coroner of Bradford (22 October 1888) and Miriam Howells of Aberdare (24 November 1888) were both found guilty.

A much quoted passage from R. Thurston Hopkins' 1935 book *Life and Death at the Old Bailey* has been quoted several times in books and websites since the 1995 publication of the Littlechild-Sims letter, to support the view that Bulling was the 'Dear Boss' author. Thurston Hopkins was a prolific writer of topographical works, ghost stories and biographies. In chapter 8, entitled 'Shadowing the Shadow of a Murderer' he discusses the Ripper case, and as a brief precursor, refers to the 'Dear Boss' letter:

But, first of all, who christened the phantom killer with the terrible soubriquet of Jack the Ripper? That is a small mystery in itself. Possibly Scotland Yard gave the name to the press and public. At that time the police post-bag bulged with hundreds of anonymous letters from all kinds of cranks and half-witted persons, who sought to criticise or hoax the officers engaged in following up the murders it was in a letter, received by a well-known news Agency and forwarded to the Yard that the name first appeared. The Criminal Investigation Department looked upon this letter as a 'clue' and possibly a message from the actual murderer. It was written in red ink, and purported to give details of the murders which had been committed. It was signed 'Jack the Ripper.' The letter was reproduced, and copies of it were fixed on the notice boards of every police station in the country, in the hope that someone would recognize the handwriting. The name, thus broadcast, 'caught on' at once.

It was perhaps a fortunate thing that the handwriting of this famous letter was perhaps not identified, for it would have led to the arrest of a harmless Fleet Street journalist. This poor fellow had a breakdown and became a whimsical figure in Fleet Street, only befriended by the staff of newspapers and printing works. He would creep about the dark courts waving his hands

furiously in the air, would utter stentorian 'Ha, ha, ha's,' and then, meeting some pal, would button-hole him and pour into his ear all the inner-story of the East End murders. Many old Fleet Streeters had very shrewd suspicions that this irresponsible fellow wrote the famous Jack the Ripper letter, and even Sir Melville L Macnaghten, Chief of the Criminal Investigation Department, had his eye on him. Sir Melville, writing in 1914, remarked: 'In this ghastly production I have always thought I could discern the stained forefinger of the journalist. Indeed, a year later, I had shrewd suspicions as to the actual author.

Thurston Hopkins, it must be said, can hardly be viewed as either a primary source, being four years old at the time of the murders, or indeed a particularly reliable one. Was this 'whimsical figure' he describes actually Bulling? While Littlechild's description of Bulling is that of an industrious man of integrity with many friends and acquaintances, prone to the occasional drink, Thurston Hopkins describes a capricious, melancholic and effusive character unrecognisable to family and friends who knew him well.

There is in fact no evidence whatsoever that his reference to the wayward journalist is rooted in any source other than Macnaghten's, of whom he freely quotes. If the embellishments, distortions and inventions which litter the rest chapter are anything to go by, his utterances with regard to the journalist are best ignored. It is rare if ever that Thurston Hopkins' other far-fetched pronouncements on the murders are quoted at length by anyone wishing to use him as a source to substantiate the Bulling notion. This is hardly surprising, as his catalogue of erroneous assertions gives no warranty whatever to the reliability of his claims about 'the poor fellow.'

Bulling died from pneumonia at the ripe old age of eighty-seven in June 1934. John Moore, the Chairman of the Central News Agency was not so fortunate. He died of tuberculosis in August 1916 at the age of sixty-four. Those who support the view that Bulling or Moore were behind the 'Dear Boss' episode proffer that their motive was financial in that Central News would gain from selling more syndicated stories as a result of the correspondence. While Central News certainly benefited along with every other news outlet covering the story, by passing it to the police before publishing it themselves, they lost the initiative and the opportunity of further exploiting it; Within days the police, as one might expect them to, released it for all to see and report on.

Bulling certainly had a reputation for a drink, but then, with no disrespect to the journalistic profession, so did countless others then and now. Neither Bulling nor Moore had, in the words of the *Daily Telegraph* 'mixed with our cousins on the other side of the Atlantic' prior to the murders.

If the police had genuine grounds to suspect either Bulling or Moore at the time, then they would clearly have sought a handwriting expert to give a view on both individuals. If they did, then any such analysis would no doubt have proved negative. Both Bulling and Moore's handwriting has been re-tested in 2009 by one of Britain's leading handwriting experts, Elaine Quigley.

This was done as part of a wider exercise for the Channel 5 documentary, *Jack the Ripper: Tabloid Killer*. Handwriting samples were sought and analysed in respect to a range of individuals, particularly journalists, some of whom had been suspected in the past of authoring the 'Dear Boss' letter. With this in mind, were there perhaps journalists with a stronger motive than Bulling or Moore? Was there a man who had, prior to the murders, spent time on the other side of the Atlantic soaking up the culture and slang of everyday Americans?

Michelle Dresbold of the United States Secret Service's Advanced Document Examination Program is one of America's top experts on handwriting and has studied the 'Dear Boss' letter for clues as to its structure and the type of individual who wrote it:

> The writer of the "Dear Boss" letter had an organised, neat, and flowing script. It is the writing of a rational, educated, and organised writer, whose actions were well thought out and planned. His i dots were well formed and always placed neatly and precisely above the stem. Exact i dots show that the writer was precise, particular, and had an eye for detail.
>
> The 'Dear Boss' author made his o's and a's clearly and crisply, with absolutely no clutter inside them. These exceptionally clean o's and a's show that the writer was a skilled communicator.
>
> The personality characteristics evident in the handwriting of the 'Dear Boss' letter are the opposite of what we would expect in the handwriting of a disorganised lust murder. However, they do fit an organised, ambitious, detail-oriented writer, someone sharp enough to pull off a hoax that could fool people for over 100 years. Could the author have been a professional writer?

Of those handwriting samples acquired and studied for the Channel 5 documentary, one in particular seemed to stand out. This was written by Frederick Best, the freelance jobbing journalist who had worked under Ernest Parke at the *Star*. The example here dates to the late 1890s when one of Best's sinecures was as a correspondent in London for a French news agency.

Elaine Quigley drew the following conclusions on it:

> The overview gives clear indication of the slant and rhythm of the two scripts, with the slant having much the same rightward angle and the letter shapes matching closely. Not only that, but the spacing between the words matches and so does the spacing between the lines, which in both cases dovetail without tangling. This is a feature seen in the writing of those who need to work under pressure and stay in control.

> Looking at the two samples it is clear that Frederick Best's sample has more flowing movement, but that of the 'Dear Boss' letter is the copybook style of the time and it also shows the care and attention to detail that was used in writing a clear and unemotional piece with which the writer did not identify.

> This can be seen in the signature, which is totally unemotional and matches the text, not what one would expect from a passionate

Jack the Ripper

and angry murderer. Not only that but the writer of the letter obviously did not identify with the name, as he did not complete the word 'Ripper' smoothly, adding the final 'r' almost as an afterthought.

Jack the Ripper

The 'staged' style of the letter could have been written out in advance and then copied., which would allow for this blip in signing the name and also for the slightly larger word spacing as attention was transferred to the draft and back to the page being written.

The script itself is slow and careful; the i-dots are neatly in place and the straight and firm baselines of the writing show a calm and dispassionate manner, certainly not the writing of an angry and emotional man. Having established the tempo of the thinking that produced this letter, let us look at the structure of the individual parts of it.

An acetate copy of the 'Dear Boss' letter was made and features on it were fitted over various similar items in the letter written by Frederick Best. Not always the same letter but the same movement was used for comparison and, as the idiosyncratic pen flow that each person makes will have its own rhythm, it is to be expected that this will be recognizable within the written trace made by that person.

New. Wil. Moon

The upper case 'N' from the Dear Boss letter fitted over the upper case letters very neatly. The letters 'a' and 'd' are also made in a similar fashion in both samples with the same dimensions.

a a a a d d d d

The letter 'e' is made with the same movement, even though the Dear Boss careful copybook is more precisely executed.

e e e e en

The letter 'f' was a particularly good fit. The Dear Boss excerpts on the left match neatly with the Frederick Best letters. Although they vary, the constant is the simplified right slanted stroke and the saucer shaped cross in the centre.

fis if f ff

The double 'l' and the 'bl' slant and are shaped, in a similar fashion between the samples, the difference in the top position of the double 'l' could be down to the difference in the mental approach at the time of writing. The note by Frederick Best would have been a natural movement, but copying a created letter under pressure both physically and emotionally, would have caused him to reverse the emphasis to reflect his feelings at the time. The left hand point being higher shows confidence and self reliance.

ll ll bl

With letter 'm', notice the tendency for the middle down stroke to move towards the left, in both the Best and 'Dear Boss' letters.

The letter 'n' also has a similar movement.

The letters 'r' 's' and 't' have a similar structure in both samples.

Throughout the Dear Boss letter and the Frederick Best letter, there are consistencies in slant, style and size, but a clinching feature is the number 5, which has a clear shape and which matches closely with both of the items.

In conclusion, Elaine Quigley commented that; 'After careful consideration, I am as sure as I can be. I really do not think that it's anyone other than Best that wrote the 'Dear Boss' letter.' If Best was the author of the 'Dear Boss' correspondence, then it is highly likely, as Elaine Quigley suggests in her analysis, that he was doing so at the behest of someone else higher up the *Star's* food-chain, who had perhaps already written out the text for him to copy, or had worked on it with him.

So far as the Americanisms used in the text of the 'Dear Boss' letter are concerned, Best's family were of the belief that he had spent a period of time working in the USA during the 1880s. A recent thorough search of US immigration and labour records initiated by the Channel 5 documentary revealed that Best had indeed been in America and had returned to Britain some months before the *Star* was launched in January 1888. In fact, Best was the only 'Dear Boss' suspect who had visited America prior to 1888.

Certainly it is impossible to conceive of a situation whereby the editor, T.P. O'Connor, would have been outside the loop. He would have at least been aware of, if not a willing participant, in the hoax. We already know from previous episodes in his career that he was not above such things. In 1871, for example, he had played a key role in the *Telegraph's* fabricated war correspondent reports. Bearing in mind that Best was at the very bottom of the *Star* hierarchy, it is questionable as to whether he would embark on such an initiative at his own behest. If he had received a helping hand from anyone, or was acting on the instructions of someone else, then Ernest Parke would be a prime suspect. Best worked closely with him on the Whitechapel Murders, providing raw material in the form of gossip, interviews and news gathering for the feature and headline stories Parke wrote for the paper. Assistant editor Henry Massingham, although seemingly having little to do with the Whitechapel murder stories was known to be fond of what he called the 'ha-ha' style of writing, reminiscent of the 'Dear Boss' style, and had written a number of private letters in a similar vein.

While O'Connor was almost certainly aware of what had happened, the fact that from the very start he seemed to have a strategy in place to safeguard his own back further implicates him. It has already been noted that he was particularly hostile towards the Central News Agency, partly due the circumstances surrounding his dismissal by them some years previously, but equally on political grounds; not only were they a hard line Conservative organisation, often seen as the party's mouthpiece, opposing the very things he held dear and had set up the *Star* to fight for, but they had also incurred his anger by the line they were currently taking against his friend and party leader Charles Stewart Parnell. Their stories supporting the view that the Parnell letters published by the *Times* were genuine and not fabrications was a very emotive issue for O'Connor. What better way of paying them back, than with a dose of their own medicine?

O'Connor's policy on the 'Dear Boss' correspondence seems designed to enable him to have his cake and eat it. For example, by maintaining from the start that the correspondence was definitely a hoax (something no other paper did so equivocally), he could exploit and publicise the story, along with the rest of the press pack, while at the same time attacking Central News for giving credence to it. It is not beyond the bounds of possibility that he could even have started the Chinese whisper, they had actually fabricated it themselves.

The *Star* were also, strangely, were the first to reveal the 'Dear Boss' story, despite the fact that they were not Central News clients. O'Connor may well have calculated that by maintaining the letters were not genuine, he would be well placed to defend himself and the paper if Best was ever exposed. In such a scenario he would no doubt have maintained that Best had acted without the knowledge and authority of the paper and that this was evident from the fact he, as editor, had taken the stance he had about their authenticity. Furthermore, if he or the paper were ever charged with wasting police time or perverting the course of justice, he would argue that on the contrary, he had been virtually the only editor to urge that the police ignore them.

1. Mortuary photo of Martha Tabram.

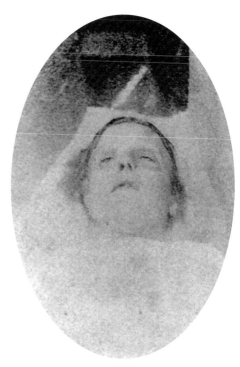

2. Mortuary photo of Mary Ann Nichols.

3. Mortuary photo of Annie Chapman;
the *Star* claimed she was the third victim of
a maniac.

4. Mortuary photo of Elizabeth Stride; already
the doctors were doubting that she had been
murdered by the same hand as Chapman.

5. A contemporary artist's impression of Elizabeth Stride in life.

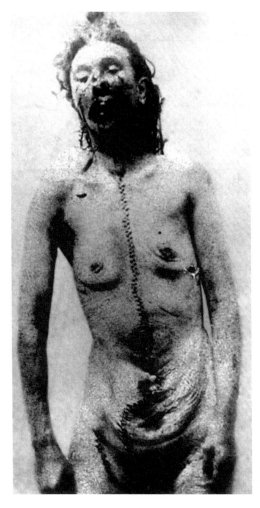

6. Catherine Eddowes after the post mortem stitching.

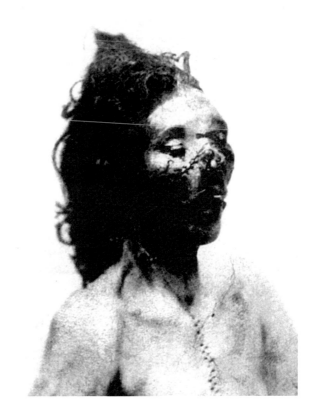

7. Catherine Eddowes' facial mutilations can be better seen in this close up.

8. Catherine Eddowes before the post mortem, the chest cavity and throat wounds are still open.

9. A contemporary artist's impression of Catherine Eddowes in life.

11. The murder scene at 13 Miller's Court; Kelly's virtually unrecognisable body lays on the bed.

A LOST WOMAN
MARY KELLY
IN MILLER'S COURT

10. A contemporary artist's impression of Kelly.

12. A mortuary photo of Alice McKenzie; her copycat murder was so similar to Nichols and Chapman, some thought she was killed by the same man.

13. A mortuary photo of Frances Coles; the police initially believed she was a victim of the Ripper.

14. An artist's impression of the discovery of Martha Tabram's body; she was most likely murdered by a soldier client.

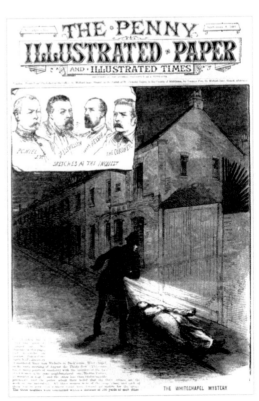

15. PC John Neil shines his bulldog lamp on the body of Mary Ann Nichols in Bucks Row.

16. 29 Hanbury Street; Annie Chapman's body was found in the back yard.

17. A rarely seen interior view of 29 Hanbury Street. Chapman and her murderer would have passed through here and out the back door to the yard.

18. Berner Street; the gates to Dutfield's Yard are below the cartwheel.

19. Louis Diemschutz discovers Elizabeth Stride's body just inside the gates of Dutfield's Yard.

20. Crowds gathering at the murder scene outside Dutfield's yard.

21. Goulston Street; the murderer threw down part of Eddowes' apron in this doorway, but did he stop to write the graffiti?

22. Artist's impression of where Eddowes'
body was found in Mitre square.

23. Mitre Square showing the entrance
from Mitre street, X marks the spot of the
murder.

24. A rarely seen illustration of the interior of 13 Miller's Court.

25. The window through which Thomas Bowyer first saw the sickening sight of Mary Kelly's body.

26. *Left*, exterior of 26 Dorset Street shortly before it was demolished in 1928, showing the entrance to Millers Court.

VICTIM
KELLY

IS HE THE
MURDERER?

27. *Right*, an artist's impression of the man described by George Hutchinson.

THE·WHITECHAPEL MONSTER SEEN BY TWO MEN.

28. *Above*, Joseph Lawende had the closest view of Eddowes' murderer when he passed the couple at the top of Church Passage. Within minutes Eddowes would be dead.
29. *Below left*, Joseph Barnett, one of Mary Kelly's male friends and a possible suspect.
30. *Below right*, Michael Kidney, Elizabeth Stride's abusive partner. She had him charged with assault in 1887.

J BARNETT
THE FRIEND OF THE
DECEASED

March 16

Dear W Evans,

I think it my becoming that as first spuel should be made to my own countymen and my own constituents. I am to address the

31. A note from T.P. O'Connor.

We are sending off some books to-day, but nothing in the way of pure literature has come our way for a long time. I suppose the book world will begin to get a bit busier now

32. A note from Ernest Parke's *Star* memo pad.

Furthermore, Mr. Best's attempt to mislead Central News during the Whitechapel Murders should have led to an earlier termination of his association with the newspaper.

I shall be glad to receive the favour of your reply, advising me of your intentions with regard to the other editorial matters previously discussed.

Yours faithfully

John J. Brunner, Esq., M.P.

33. In Brunner's letter to Henry Massingham he refers to his unhappiness over the 'Best' episode.

34. Ernest Parke, the feature writer who crafted the *Star's* Ripper stories.

35. Henry Massingham, Assistant Editor of the *Star* and the man who aided the proprietors in removing O'Connor from the helm.

36. T.P. O'Connor, the creator of the 'single serial killer' and the greatest newspaper headline of all time; 'Jack the Ripper'.

37. John Brunner, one the *Star's* proprietors who eventually lost patience with O'Connor's 'vulgar' journalism.

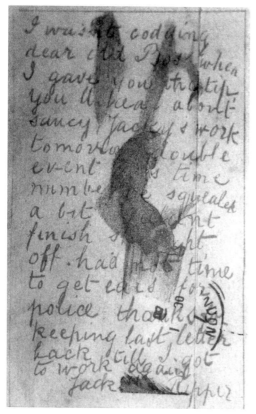

THE CENTRAL NEWS LIMITED

5. New Bridge Street.

London 29 Sep 1888

E.C.

The Editor presents his compliments to Mr Williamson & begs to inform him the Enclosed was sent the Central news two days ago, & was treated as a joke.

38. Thomas Bulling's covering note to Scotland Yard which accompanied the 'Dear Boss' letter.

I was not codding dear old Boss when I gave you the tip. you'll hear about saucy Jacky's work tomorrow double event this time number one squealed a bit couldn't finish straight off. had not time to get ears for police. thanks for keeping last letter back till I got to work again. Jack the Ripper

39. The 'Dear Boss' letter was quickly followed by a postcard from the same writer.

From hell

Mr Lusk

Sor

I send you half the
Kidne I took from one women
prasarved it for you tother pieci
fried and ate it was very nise I
may send you the bloody knif that
took it out if you only wate a whil
longer

Signed   Catch me when
          you can
          Mishter Lusk

40. The 'From Hell' letter to George Lusk which accompanied the half kidney. Was it a medical student's prank?

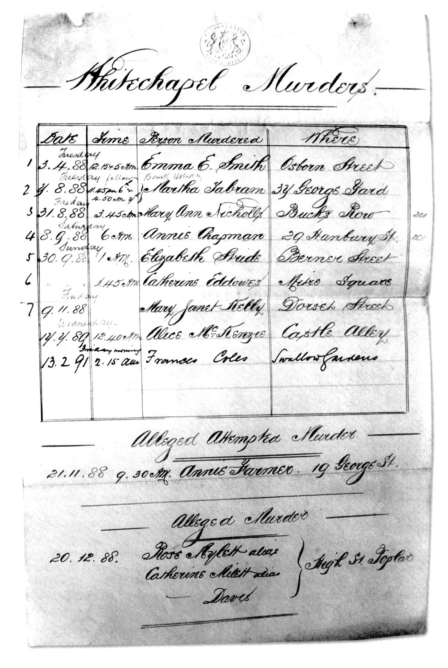

Whitechapel Murders

	Date	Time	Person Murdered	Where	
1	Tuesday 3.4.88	12.15+5 am	Emma E. Smith	Osborn Street	
2	Tuesday following 7.8.88	1.45 am 6½ am 4.50 am	Martha Tabram Bank Holiday	37 Georges Yard	
3	Friday 31.8.88	3.45 am	Mary Ann Nicholls	Bucks Row	201
4	Saturday 8.9.88	6 am	Annie Chapman	29 Hanbury St.	201
5	Sunday 30.9.88	1 am	Elizabeth Stride	Berner Street	
6	" "	1.45 am	Catherine Eddowes	Mitre Square	
7	Friday 9.11.88		Mary Janet Kelly	Dorset Street	
	Wednesday 17.4.89	12.40 am	Alice McKenzie	Castle Alley	
	Friday morning 13.2.91	2.15 am	Frances Coles	Swallow Gardens	

— Alleged Attempted Murder —

21.11.88 9.30 am Annie Farmer. 19 George St.

— Alleged Murder —

20.12.88. Rose Mylett alias Catherine Millett alias — Davis } High St. Poplar

42. A contemporary police list of the Whitechapel murder victims.

41. The Whitechapel Murder files at Scotland Yard, prior to their public release and transfer to the National Archive.

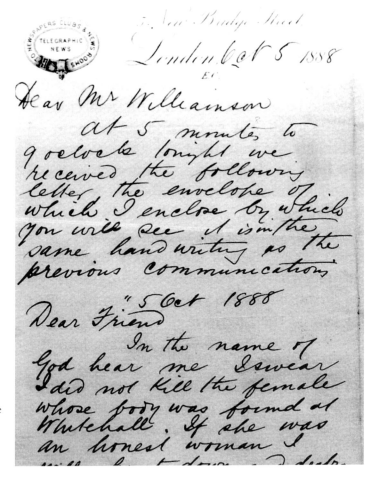

THE CENTRAL NEWS LIMITED.

TELEGRAPHIC NEWS

London Oct 5 1888

Dear Mr Williamson
        At 5 minutes to
9 oclock tonight we
received the following
letter, the envelope of
which I enclose by which
you will see it is in the
same hand writing as the
previous communications

            "5 Oct 1888
Dear Friend
            In the name of
God hear me I swear
I did not kill the female
whose body was found at
Whitehall. If she was
an honest woman I

43. Thomas Bulling's controversial letter concerning the third letter from the 'Dear Boss' author. Why did he not enclose it with this covering note?

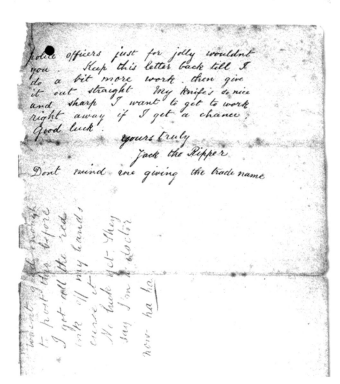

25. Sept. 1888.

Dear Boss

I keep on hearing the police
have caught me. but they wont fix
me just yet. I have laughed when
they look so clever and talk about
being on the right track. That joke
about Leather apron gave me real
fits. I am down on whores and
I shant quit ripping them till I
do get buckled. Grand work the last
job was. I gave the lady no time to
squeal. How can they catch me now.
I love my work and want to start
again. You will soon hear of me
with my funny little games. I
saved some of the proper red stuff in
a ginger beer bottle over the last job
to write with but it went thick
like glue and I cant use it. Red
ink is fit enough I hope ha. ha.
The next job I do I shall clip
the ladys ears off and send to the

44. The 'Dear Boss' letter,
page one.

police officers just for jolly wouldnt
you. Keep this letter back till I
do a bit more work. then give
it out straight My knifes so nice
and sharp I want to get to work
right away if I get a chance.
Good luck.
            yours truly
                Jack the Ripper
Dont mind me giving the trade name

wasnt good enough
to post this before
I got all the red
ink off my hands
curse it
No luck yet. They
say I am a doctor
now ha ha

45. The 'Dear Boss' letter, page two.

The case, referred to in the sensational story told in "the Sun" in its issue of 13th inst, or following dates, is that of Thomas Cutbush who was arraigned at the London County Sessions in April 1891, on a charge of maliciously wounding Florence Grace Johnson, & attempting to wound Isabella Fraser Anderson in Kennington. He was found to be insane, and sentenced to be detained during Her Majesty's pleasure.

46. The famous Macnaghten memo was sparked off by T.P. O'Connor's five day Ripper revelation in the *Sun* between 14 and 18 February 1894.

47. The *Star* exploited the Ripper story primarily through its street seller billboards.

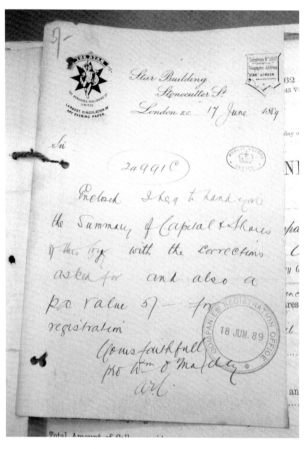

48. The only way the proprietors could break O'Connor's grip on the editor's chair was to dissolve the company that owned the *Star* and create a brand new one.

49. *Below left*, Sir Robert Anderson, the controversial Assistant Commissioner of the Metropolitan Police. How much of his retrospective Ripper recollections were faulty memory, and how much was fabrication?

50. *Below right*, Dr George Bagster Phillips; he and Dr Clark withheld vital medical details from the inquests.

51. Sir Melville Macnaghten, the man who created the 'five victims' theory.

52. Dr Percy Clark, who along with Dr Phillips knew more about the medical aspects of the murders than anyone else.

"THE COMPANIES ACTS, 1862 to 1883."

25 & 26th Vict. c. 89, 30th & 31st Vict. c. 131, 40th & 41st Vict. c. 26, 42 & 43rd Vict. c. 76, 43rd Vict. c. 19, and 46th & 47th Vict. c. 28).

COMPANY LIMITED BY SHARES.

(COPY.)

Special Resolutions

(Pursuant to Companies Act, 1862, ss. 50 & 51)

OF THE

CENTRAL NEWS LIMITED.

Passed the 12th day of June, 1886. Confirmed the 3rd day of July, 1886.

At an Extraordinary General Meeting of the Members of the said Company, duly convened, and held at the Company's Offices, 5, New Bridge Street, Blackfriars, in the City of London, on the 12th day of June, 1886, the following Special Resolutions were duly passed; and at a subsequent Extraordinary General Meeting of the Members of the said Company, also duly convened, and held at the same place, on the 3rd day of July, 1886, the following Special Resolutions were duly confirmed:—

RESOLVED—

1. That the Capital of the Company be increased to £24,000, by the creation of 200 New Shares of £20 each.

2. That the Directors be and they are hereby authorised to issue 150 of such New Shares to the persons and in the proportions specified in the Provisional Agreement, dated the 14th day of May, 1886, made between the Company of the one part, and John Moore, Alfred Kinnear, John Gennings, John Lanyon, William Forbes, Alfred Sanderson, Thomas John Bulling, Charles Dickenson, and Charles Baker of the other part, to be submitted to the said above-mentioned Extraordinary General Meeting, and without being bound to offer the same, or any of them, to existing members of the Company, and that such Shares be respectively credited in the books of the Company as fully paid-up Shares.

3. That the Directors be and they are hereby authorised to issue the remainder of such New Shares, or any of them, at any time, or from time to time, to such person or persons, in such proportions and upon such terms as to payment by instalments or otherwise, or as fully or partially paid-up Shares, and for such consideration, either past, present, or future, or without any valuable consideration, as they may think fit, and without being bound to offer the same, or any of them, to existing members for the time being of the Company.

4. That the following alterations be made in the Articles of Association of the Company, and that henceforth the Articles of Association be read and construed as if the words proposed to be omitted were not included therein.

In Clause 10 omit the words "other than the said William Saunders, his executors or administrators," in the first and second lines; the words "without the consent in writing of the said William Saunders so long as he shall continue a member of the

53. In 1886 Thomas Bulling became a dirctor and shareholder in Central News Ltd. His role in the 'Dear Boss' saga is a contentious one.

Finally, as we saw in the previous chapter, although the *Star* reproduced the wording of the 'Dear Boss' correspondence and exploited the Jack the Ripper name on its billboards, it strangely took a hard line against the *Telegraph* when they reproduced the actual handwriting. O'Connor's objection was supposedly on grounds of public taste, which was a little rich coming from the paper that had, more than any other, peddled the ghoulish aspects of the story to the full. Was it perhaps the case that there was a worry that someone, somewhere, might recognise the handwriting?

It is unknown how much police time was expended in dealing with the 'Dear Boss' correspondence, and the avalanche of three hundred plus letters which were posted subsequently as a direct result, by other copycat hoaxers. Without doubt this escapade diverted valuable police time and funds from pursuing the real killer.

As already noted, although Anderson and Macnaghten stated many years later that they suspected a hoax, it is clear that DCI Henry Moore, who had taken over the Ripper case from Inspector Abberline, certainly thought they were genuine. We also know that nearly a century later another very similar hoax diverted a police murder investigation into a blind alley and allowed the real killer to be initially eliminated from suspicion.

On 20 October 2005, police arrested fifty year old John Humble in Sunderland. Under questioning he admitted that he was the notorious 'Wearside Jack' who sent three hoax letters and an audio tape that diverted police hunting the Yorkshire Ripper in 1978. However, he denied four counts of intending to pervert the course of justice when he appeared at Leeds Crown Court on 9 January 2006. Found guilty, he was sentenced to eight years in jail on 21 March 2006.

Although the original letters had been destroyed by chemicals used in fingerprint tests to identify the author, a genetic profile was established from saliva on parts of envelopes. The letters and tape, posted in Sunderland, between March 1978 and June 1979, persuaded police to consider only men with Geordie or Wearside accents as Ripper suspects. During that time Peter Sutcliffe, jailed for life in May 1981 after admitting thirteen murders, claimed a further three victims. Sutcliffe had been questioned several times but was eliminated because of his West Yorkshire accent.

Two of the hoax letters were sent to Assistant Chief constable George Oldfield, who led the serial murder inquiry. A third was sent to the *Daily Mirror* newspaper. Mr Oldfield made the tape public, and millions listened spellbound as it was broadcast on television and radio. The hoax prompted a huge effort by police in the Wearside area with campaigns for people to come forward if they recognised the voice or writing. Linguistic experts said the taped voice possessed local Sunderland characteristics, 'suggesting the area of origin was small and it was highly likely the person would be identified and quickly'.

A later report on the police investigation said, 'Arguments will rage for years as to why the letters and tape were regarded as authentic. They totally misled the investigation.'

Retired Detective Superintendent Dick Holland, seventy-two, who worked on the Ripper inquiry commented that, 'we accepted the tape and letters as genuine because it had information we felt was only privy to the murder.' At Humble's trial, the prosecution told the judge that prior to Sutcliffe's arrest; some half a million police man hours, and over £1,000,000 had been taken up in trying to identify 'Wearside Jack.'

In the same way that aspects of the 'Dear Boss' correspondence were erroneously thought to be privy only to the murderer, another letter, accompanying a small bloodstained box containing half a human kidney, would shortly be in the hands of the Whitechapel investigators. Was this yet another hoax or was this a genuine communication from the murderer of Catherine Eddowes?

CHAPTER 6

CANNIBAL RIPPER

The deaths of Elizabeth Stride and Catherine Eddowes attracted a huge amount of press coverage during the week following their murders. Plagiarism amongst newspapers was very much in evidence as a result of syndicated news and the fact that some evening newspapers would 'take' information from the morning newspapers, and the Sunday papers 'picked' from the daily newspapers. Therefore, witness accounts, interviews and general features would have a very similar tone and outlook.

The *Star*, as we have already seen was in many ways unique in the sense that it hardly ever used syndicated news and had a second to none grassroots newsgathering operation which fed writers like Ernest Parke. On 1 October he wrote a front-page story of several columns in length which gave explicit detail underneath a manifold headline, part of which read:

THE MURDER MANIAC SACRIFICES MORE WOMEN TO
HIS THIRST FOR BLOOD

This article concentrated on the viciousness of the murders and how these events had sent 'a thrill of horror throughout the land.'

This time the 'hellish fiend who stalks abroad in Whitechapel' had struck down two 'poor unfortunate and degraded women.' After virtually beheading his first victim, he had gone on to Mitre Square where he 'hacked, mutilated, and disembowelled' his victim. He quoted PC Watkins as stating that when he found the body of Catherine Eddowes 'her clothing had been thrown up breast-high,' her stomach 'ripped up like a pig in the market,' and her entrails 'flung in a heap around her neck.' Parke also asserted his belief at the time that, 'the abdomen had been ripped open and the puberic [sic] bone left completely bare, no part of the body was missing.'

In a further article, he addressed the issue of escalating uneasiness in Whitechapel, where the police had closed every entrance to the sites where the murders took place and were ordering the spectators to keep moving.

On the same date, in a somewhat hypocritical appeal, the *Star* pleaded with journalists when writing about the carnage to 'keep their heads cool and not inflame men's passions.' One of its leaders about the murders described the people of Whitechapel as 'half-mad with fear.' Parke openly dismissed the theory by Coroner Baxter that an American pathologist had employed someone to acquire uteruses for the purposes of medical research. He also conjectured that the murderer had undergone an 'epileptic outbreak of homicidal mania.' This was followed by his call to bring light to the people of Whitechapel without delay, to avoid the start of an uprising that would 'smash the Empire' and herald the start of a republican administration.

On the 2 October the *Star* criticised the 'moral crusades' of West End reformers accusing them of being ineffective. Parke felt most of the problems of Whitechapel were caused by 'eighteen hundred years of Christian civilisation.' He felt one could argue,

that the only alternative on offer to life in the slums, was death. His answer therefore, was to give the people bright lights and fresh air. A political battle culminating in the eradication of slumlords and unfair taxes meant people would be forced to choose between 'Terror' and 'Reason'.

Scotland Yard did not provide details as to the methods they were using to find the Ripper. In the absence of this information, the papers had to rely on printing details about the inquests, details of the reward money, the actions of the vigilance committees, the continuing nervousness in Whitechapel, and the detaining and discharging of suspects. Also considered newsworthy, was the complaints by prostitutes of the risk attached to their nightly line of work. These competed for consideration, alongside alleged clues concerning the Ripper.

In particular, the press fixed its attention on providing prolonged extracts from the five sessions of the Stride inquest and the four sessions of the Eddowes's inquest. Relying on sensationalising and drawing on the horror of these extracts, much time was spent discussing Eddowes's injuries, emphasising as Parke did on the Ripper's 'insensate desire to disfigure the face' and the 'wanton and unnatural delight' he took in mutilating her body.

A few papers used the murders as an opportunity to focus on the moral and social issues of the country, to look at and promote the welfare and needs of the nation, rather than concentrating on its enforcing of the law. The Rev Samuel Barnett was given the opportunity by the *Star*, on the 5 October, under the headline 'The Moral of the Murders' to express his opinion about the fundamental causes of the killings. His stance was that both the rich and the working class were responsible for the miserable plight of the poor. He charged reputable husbands with controlling and badly treating their wives and working-class men of ill-treating their women. The lack of equality between men and women at home and in the workplace meant women would always be at the hands of men who were exempt from punishment. If men ever admitted that this abuse was worse than the killing of six ill-fated women then sexual equality might transpire and England would be a happier place. Meanwhile, the answer lay in people looking out for each other and being aware of the crimes and abuse going on around them. The rich should fund better lighting and housing for the underprivileged and the latter should respect their women and love their fellow citizens.

Once the two inquests were concluded, and in the absence of any further murders, journalists were compelled to concentrate on circumstances in the East End. Principally their focus was on the associations between gentiles and Jews, the filth and unpleasantness of lodging houses, the criminal component, the necessity of streetlights, the subculture of unfortunates, and the despondent state of trade.

The *Star*, always keen to acquire a story out of the ordinary, published on the 6 October an account given to them by a doctor who had recently called at Stonecutter Street and spoken with O'Connor and Parke. He told them about a former surgical assistant of his who had previously worked in Whitechapel and whom had contracted a venereal infection. In his opinion this depraved man would single-mindedly be seeking to take revenge on all prostitutes, to castigate them for his misfortune. Importantly, this man knew in detail the Whitechapel area. The doctor condemned the police for treating him in an offhanded manner when he voiced his concerns.

Commissioner Warren's decision to eradicate with a sponge, the chalk writing in Goulston Street, which a number of papers quickly alleged to be an authentic clue left by the murderer, gave the dailies on the 8 and 9 October the opportunity to create some outrage.

The writing and part of Catherine Eddowes' apron had been found some two hours after her murder by PC Alfred Long:

> I was on duty in Goulston Street on the morning of 30th September at about 2.55 am. I found a portion of an apron covered in blood lying in the passage of the door-way leading to nos. 108 to 119 Model Dwellings in Goulston Street.
>
> Above it on the wall was written in chalk 'The Juews are the men that will not be blamed fir nothing.' I at once called the PC on the adjoining beat and then searched the stair-cases, but found no traces of any person or marks. I at once proceeded to the station, telling the PC to see that no one entered or left the building in my absence. I arrived at the station about 5 or 10 minutes past 3, and reported to the Inspector on duty finding the apron and the writing.
>
> The Inspector at once proceeded to Goulston Street and inspected the writing. From there we proceeded to Lemen Street, and the apron was handed by the Inspector to a gentleman whom I have since learnt is Dr Phillips. I then returned back on duty in Goulston Street about 5.

Contrary to popular belief, it was actually Superintendent Arnold's suggestion to wipe out the graffiti, as:

> I was apprehensive that if the writing were left it would be the means of causing a riot and therefore considered it desirable that it should be removed.

Warren, who was at the scene with Arnold certainly approved it, for reasons he outlined in a communication with the Home Office on 6 November:

> The most pressing question at the moment was some writing on the wall in Goulston Street evidently written with the intention of inflaming the public mind against the Jews, and which Mr Arnold with a view to prevent serious disorder proposed to obliterate it, and had sent down an Inspector with a sponge for that purpose telling him to await his arrival. I considered it desirable that I should decide this matter myself, as it was one involving so great a responsibility whether any action was taken or not.

Despite the attention the Goulston Street graffiti attracted in the press, its relevancy as evidence is very much open to question. Chalk graffiti on the street and in passageways such as this was widespread. The likelyhood was that the killer had gone down Goulston Street as he fled from Mitre Square around 1.50 a.m. or thereabouts and had randomly thrown down the piece of apron in a doorway. Had he discarded it two doorways before 108-119 or three doorways after 108-119, the graffiti found near or above the discarded apron would have been entirely different. As it is, many modern Ripper writers have debated endlessly about the graffiti's possible Masonic meaning, due to the misspelling of the word 'Juwes', which they have associated with Jubelo, Jubela and Jubelum, the mythical Masonic murderers of the master-mason of King Solomon's Temple. The graffiti is far more likely to be the work of an anti Semitic east-ender, who had a problem with spelling.

The Goulson Street message also raised to the surface the underlying tension of anti-Semitism. Suspects were hunted for by the police, amongst young Jewish males, in particular those of a dark facial appearance with black hair and a beard. This general description did of course undoubtedly match many residents of the East End, even if some of the suspects, with their sandy moustaches or fair skin colouring did not fit into this category.

Letters published by the press expressed the view that the Ripper was a ritual killer who was an authority on cutting animals' throats. They therefore, believed the murder weapon was a knife used for these activities by 'Jewish cutters.' With readers being reminded about shocking tales of Jewish ritual killings in Eastern Europe it was not forgotten that Stride's murder took place behind the back entrance to a Jewish working-class club and the graffiti found on Goulston Street was about the 'Juwes.'

There was a gradual petering out of information concerning the Ripper as October wore on. Towards the end of October when lack of information could easily have led to the demise of the Ripper story, the Liberal and Radical press chose to focus on the need for improvements in the living conditions of people in the East End. The destructive effects of poor standards of living were, it was suggested, to blame for the murders. The answer was social change induced by the funding of street lighting, housing and provision for the homeless.

The waning narrative of the exploits of Jack the Ripper received a revival when in answer to the reader's curiosity regarding the whereabouts of the body parts removed from Chapman and Eddowes, a half of a human kidney was received, in a bloodstained box, by George Lusk, co-founder of the Whitechapel Vigilance Committee. Accompanying the parcel was a rough and ready note:

From Hell. Mr Lusk. Sir, - I send you half a kidne I took from one woman, prasarved it for you, tother piece I fried and ate it; was very nice. I may send you the bloody knif that took it out if you only wate while longer. (signed) 'Catch me when you can.' Mr Lusk.

Scotland Yard's response was a wall of silence which only gave more credence to the incident. The press made the most of this latest horror to renew interest in the continuing saga and unhesitatingly credited it to the Ripper. A typical headline was to be found on 19 October in the *Evening News*, 'Half The Victim's Missing Kidney Restored – The Other Half Eaten by Cannibal Assassin.' Not to be outdone, the *Star* ran its own kidney story the same day and used its advertising billboards to proclaim, 'Cannibal Ripper.'

The press were, on the whole, divided on their portrayal of the 'kidney' incident. Although it was a valuable tool for sensation-horror, it was played down by several papers, including the *East End News* of 19 October, which chose to take no notice of the event, possibly because either local cannibalism was too vulgar a concept to contemplate or they considered the whole incident to be a hoax. The main newspaper of the Jewish community, the Jewish Chronicle, had not even made reference to the Nichols and Chapman killings, until the accusation that the murderer was possibly a kosher butcher became widespread.

On the same day, the *Star* carried an update on the 'kidney story':

Easy to Hoax the Police - The Kidney Story.

As a motive for the disgusting hoax of the kidney, it is suggested that the person who sent it to its recipient desired to keep up the excitement about the crimes. We are now informed that the information of the receipt of the parcel was sold at a high figure, so that the hoax does not appear so stupid as it seemed at first.

Like the Goulston Street graffiti, the kidney story has now taken on almost mythical proportions. In countless books and films the claim has been made that Catherine Eddowes had Bright's disease, a term used in 1888 to describe an inflammation of the kidneys brought about by excessive alcohol consumption.

Dr Thomas Openshaw, who had examined the kidney at the London Hospital, was quoted in the *Telegraph* on 19 October as concluding that it was the left kidney of a female and furthermore that it was a 'ginny kidney.' However, not only did Openshaw repudiate this story and deny that this was what he had said, he clarified the position in an interview in the *Star* which was published later the same day:

> Dr Openshaw told a Star reporter today that having examined the piece of kidney under the microscope he was of the opinion that it was half of a left human kidney. He couldn't say, however, whether it was that of a woman, nor how long it had been removed from the body, as it has been preserved in spirits.

In spite of this, many now believe without question that it was in fact Eddowes' kidney and by implication in the validity of the accompanying letter from the killer. While the *Telegraph* story was undoubtedly the foundation on which this particular myth was born, it was Lieutenant-Colonel Sir Henry Smith, the former

Commissioner of the City of London police, who took it one major step further. Smith, a man who had a minimal involvement in the Whitechapel murders, had, like Sir Robert Anderson, an autobiography to promote in 1910 - 'From Constable to Commissioner.' In it he waxes lyrical about the kidney incident:

When the body was examined by the police surgeon, Mr Gordon Brown, one kidney was found to be missing, and some days after the murder what purported to be that kidney was posted to the office of the Central News, together with a short note of rather a jocular character unfit for publication. Both kidney and note the manager at once forwarded to me. Unfortunately, as always happens, some clerk or assistant in the office was got at, and the whole affair was public property next morning. Right royally did the Solons of the metropolis enjoy themselves at the expense of my humble self and the City Police Force. "The kidney was the kidney of a dog, anyone could see that," wrote one. "Evidently from the dissecting-room," wrote another. "Taken out of a corpse after a post mortem," wrote a third. "A transparent hoax," wrote a fourth. My readers shall judge between myself and the Solons in question.

I made over the kidney to the police surgeon, instructing him to consult with the most eminent men in the profession, and send me a report without delay. I give the substance of it. The renal artery is about three inches long. Two inches remained in the corpse; one inch was attached to the kidney. The kidney left in the corpse was in an advanced stage of Bright's disease; the kidney sent me was in an exactly similar state. But what was of far more importance, Mr. Sutton, one of the senior surgeons of the London Hospital,

whom Gordon Brown asked to meet him and another practitioner
in consolation, and who was one of the greatest authorities living
on the kidney and its diseases, said he would pledge his reputation
that the kidney submitted to them had been put in spirits within a
few hours of its removal from the body - thus effectually disposing
of all hoaxes in connection with it. The body of anyone done to
death by violence is not taken direct to the dissecting room, but
must await an inquest, never held before the following day at the
soonest.

While one can be charitable in attributing most of the errors in the
above account to the lapse in memory of an old man, Smith was,
without doubt, trying to give the impression that he had been at the
centre of the Ripper drama, and had no qualms about re-writing
history to make this appear to have been so.

Apart from beginning his account by borrowing from the 'Dear
Boss' story and claiming that the kidney and letter were sent
to Central News and then relayed to him by the Central News
manager, he goes on to make a number of statements that he must
have known full well were simply untrue. For example, when Dr
Brown was interviewed by the *Sunday Times* (21 October 1888),
he stated that the renal artery had been trimmed off, in other words
two inches did not remain in the corpse. He also stated that in his
view it was unlikely to be Eddowes' kidney. Neither did he say
at any time, either in his autopsy report or in any interview, that
Eddowes remaining kidney was in any way diseased. In fact, Dr
William Saunders, who was also at the Eddowes autopsy told the
Manchester Evening News (19 October 1888) that; 'you can take it
from me that the right kidney of the woman Eddowes was perfectly
normal in its structure and healthy.' Saunders, like many others at

the time, including George Lusk himself, believed the whole thing was a prank by a student at the London Hospital.

Interestingly, Inspector McWilliam's report of 27 October 1888 makes no reference to a Mr Sutton from the London Hospital or indeed anyone vaguely resembling, 'one of the greatest authorities living on the kidney and its diseases.' In fact, no record of a Mr Sutton has ever been found at the London Hospital.

Within days the gripping cannibal kidney story disappeared from the leading papers. Their news relating to the Ripper cases was made up from space filling stories about petty East End crime, new and existing suspects, embroidered with complaints from police constables about their onerous workload and the pressure placed upon them to make an arrest.

Within three weeks the horrendous murder of Mary Kelly occurred on 9 November, the only murder to be committed indoors at 13 Miller's Court, Dorset Street. In the hours and days following, the police showed a great unwillingness to pass on to the press news of any advances they might be making. This lack of explanation, the partial news blackout which was imposed by Scotland Yard, and the contradictory accounts by witnesses goes to offer some explanation as to why the coverage of the Kelly murder was muddled and confusing.

A sub-headline in the *Star* on the day of the murder stated the police were 'COMPLETELY BAFFLED.' It was even unclear as to whether, besides the extraction of the heart and organs from Kelly as mentioned in most papers, which body parts if any, the killer had carried away. Unbeknown to the Liberal and Radical press, Chief Commissioner Warren had submitted his resignation prior to Kelly's murder. In their unremitting opinion, amidst the inconsistencies and silences, the Kelly murder was the deciding factor in proving his sheer incompetence.

Warren and Matthews were considered to be incompetent. Would it take the murder of an eleventh or twelfth person to make them see what was happening, or compel them to tender their resignations? They had erased the only clue, (written on the wall in Goulston Street) and ruined 'the machinery for the detection of crime.' Regardless of the ethnic origin of the killer, whether he was looking for revenge or a 'debauchee gone mad with excess, possessed by a passion for blood superadded to the mere brutal instinct from which that passion spreads,' the police had been ineffectual and had failed in their duty to the public.

On 10 November the *Star* appealed to its readers to look vigilantly amongst their own friends for anyone with a profile that fitted that of the murderer, given that the killer had managed, regardless of his mental state, to avoid discovery. Perhaps he was a loner living in a city known for 'the isolation of life.' He might even be a gentleman, a churchgoer, a clerk, or a dealer in stocks and shares, whose co-workers suspected nothing. The front-page leader 'WHAT WE THINK,' blamed the Ripper's escape entirely on Warren and Matthews. While the CID was in the hands of a 'clumsy, wilful and ignorant martinet,' the Home Office had 'a heedless and helpless' man at the helm. More insults ensued. Warren and Matthews were blamed for widening the gap between the social orders of London, and it was considered that the sooner they resigned the better.

Was this really the reason the police appeared so inept in their attempts to solve the Whitechapel murders, or was there perhaps another explanation?

CHAPTER 7

COPYCAT KILLER

As we noted at the beginning of our story, the police 'Whitechapel Murders' file contained eleven victims murdered in a similar way within the broad geographical area of Whitechapel. Many people today believe that of these, five victims were murdered by the same killer. These victims have even been dubbed 'the canonical five' by Ripperologists, but where does this belief in a five victim killer come from?

The first person to state on the record that there were five victims murdered by the same killer was Sir Melville Macnaghten in his notes dated 24 February 1894:

Now the Whitechapel murderer had 5 victims - & 5 victims only, - his murders were

(1)   31st August '88. Mary Ann Nichols – at Bucks Row – who was found with her throat cut - & with (slight) stomach mutilation.

(2)   8th Sept. '88. Annie Chapman – Hanbury Street; - throat cut – stomach and priva te parts badly mutilated & some of the entrails placed round the neck.

(3)   30 th Sept. '88 Elizabeth Stride – Berner's [sic] Street – throat cut, but nothing in shape of mutilation attempted, & on same date Catherine Eddowes – Mitre Square, throat cut & very bad mutilation, both face & stomach.

9th November, Mary Jane Kelly – Miller's Court, throat cut, and the whole body mutilated in the most ghastly manner -

Macnaghten goes on to establish two further theories in his notes, that are today taken almost as gospel by Ripperologists:

> With regard to the double murder which took place on 30th September, there is no doubt but that the man was disturbed by some Jews who drove up to a Club, (close to which the body of Elizabeth Stride was found) and that he then, 'nondum satiatus', went in search of a further victim who he found in Mitre Square.

Having set down his 'five victims' theory and his consequent *'nondum satiatus'* (not yet satisfied) theory, Macnaghten goes one giant leap further:

> It will be noticed that the fury of the mutilations *increased* in each case, and, seemingly the appetite only became sharpened by indulgence.

Although he did not term it as such, this view is known today among Ripperologists as the 'escalation theory'. It is one however, that has no basis in either the study of criminology or in criminal behaviour patterns. It has been created to account for the 'ratcheting-up' of violence used. Police experience of serial murders not just in Britain and the United States but around the world, has been that serial killers retain a similar if not identical method to each murder. They do not, in other words, radically increase or decrease the amount of mutilation employed in each consecutive case.

It is worth reminding ourselves at this point that unlike today, the most senior office holders of the Metropolitan Police (and indeed other constabularies) in Victorian England were not actually trained police officers, or indeed police officers at all in the true sense of the word. The custom and practice of the day was to appoint individuals from what was perceived to be the correct social background to administer the police. Often, it seems to have been felt that senior army officers were somehow fitted to run a police force. If, for example, we look at the most senior men running the Metropolitan Police at the time of the Whitechapel murders, we find that the Commissioner, Sir Charles Warren, was a Major-General who had distinguished himself as a surveyor in the Royal Engineers. His first experience of working with or administering a police force was encountered on the first day he walked into Scotland Yard as Commissioner in 1886.

Sir James Monro, who was Assistant Commissioner and later Commissioner following Warren's resignation, had been a civil servant in the legal branch of the Indian Civil Service. Although being briefly responsible for the Bombay police in a civil service capacity he had no active police service experience. Likewise, Sir Robert Anderson, who succeeded Monro as Assistant Commissioner in August 1888 was by training a barrister who had cut his teeth on anti-Fenian intelligence work for the Home Office.

Macnaghten in this sense was no different. After leaving Eton in 1872, he went straight to Bengal to run his father's tea estates and remained there until 1888, when Assistant Commissioner James Monro recommended him for the post of first Chief Constable

(CID). Monro had been a close friend of Macnaghten's in India and his recommendation was seen by Sir Charles Warren as an example of the old pals act. He over-ruled the recommendation officially on the grounds of Macnaghten's conduct during the 1881 Indian land riots, although it seems apparent he also had grave reservations about Macnaghten's ability and suitability for the post. His decision was also indicative of the growing personal rift between Monro and Warren at the time. Monro grudgingly bided his time and appointed Macnaghten immediately he was made Commissioner in Warren's place. Essentially then, Macnaghten may have been an effective administrator of a tea estate (although even this is questionable in light of the events of 1881) but was probably the least qualified man ever to hold a senior police position in Britain before or since.

Interestingly, when Macnaghten retired from his post in 1913 he was succeeded as Assistant Commissioner (CID) by fellow old Etonian Sir Basil Thomson. He too had a personal interest in the Whitechapel Murders, and like Macnaghten took the time while in post to study the case papers in detail.

Thomson's take on the Whitechapel murders was somewhat different. In his papers he states the following on the subject of Jack the Ripper:

> The name was taken from the signature of one of the bogus letters published by the police. The victims in every case were prostitutes who were ripped up by what appeared to be surgical knives of extreme sharpness. After the second of these murders the public took alarm, and there was widespread criticism of CID.

Significantly, it would appear that he had different views from Macnaghten as to the number of victims attributed to one killer. Hedging his bets, he felt it was between '3 and 6.' Although like Macnaghten, Thomson's notes contained a number of factual errors, the essential point here is two-fold. Firstly, that the retrospective analysis conducted by both Macnaghten and Thomson, was based at the end of the day on opinion not fact. Secondly that whatever views such senior post holders took, it was in fact profoundly different from those held by the trained career police officers on the ground, who had actually been involved in the murder investigations at the time.

These officers, i.e. the superintendents, chief inspectors and inspectors, who had learnt their trade by hard earned experience from many years of policing, often put their views on record. However, these tended not to be given the same status as the utterings of their Eton educated superiors.

Superintendent Thomas Arnold, for example, who had joined the Metropolitan Police in 1855 was head of the H Whitechapel Division at the time of the murders. When he retired in 1893 he expressed regret that his division had not been successful in solving the murders, and went further on 3 February that year to state that in his view more than one killer was responsible for the five murders. As we shall see, he was not alone in differing from Macnaghten on this vital point.

Because there were so few real clues and so little real evidence, the Whitechapel murders have provided a field-day for those pushing their own pet and eccentric theories. This in turn has lead to classic examples of 'reverse research'. So many have started with their own pet theories and then researched backwards trying to make everything fit their chosen conclusion. If something doesn't quite fit in with their theory, it's either air brushed out, or a theory is contrived to get around or explain it away.

If one air-brushes out a victim or two at the beginning and end of the sequence, you're left with the so-called 'Canonical Five', as these best fit the argument for the single killer theory. However, even these do not fit when subjected to closer scrutiny.

The following points should be considered in any debate concerning whether one, two or more killers were responsible for the deaths of Mary Ann Nichols, Annie Chapman, Elizabeth Stride, Catherine Eddowes and Mary Kelly.

There were clearly differences in the five murders that lead to the possibility of multiple murderers to the extent that all five of the murders could have conceivably been committed by three, four or even five different people. The first two (of the five) victims, Nichols and Chapman, are similar, although nowhere near identical. While both were suffocated before having their throats cut, Nichols' mutilations were below the breast bone and merely exposed the intestines. In spite of a number of erroneous claims to the contrary over the years, no internal organs were taken from Nichols' body.

Chapman, on the other hand, had more extensive mutilations and the whole of the uterus, two-thirds of the bladder and the upper part of the vagina were removed. Although many newspapers claimed Nichols as the third victim (i.e. after Smith and Tabram), the Nichols inquest was the first to be reported in detail, to the extent that fine details was given in the press of the nature of the mutilations and the modus operandi of the killer.

Elizabeth Stride's murder was radically different. Neither was the murder scene typical of the type common in the cases of Nichols, Chapman and Eddowes, i.e. a lonely isolated location.

Dutfield's Yard was illuminated by the International Working Men's Educational Club windows which ran the full length of the yard. Some thirty people were estimated to have been in the club at the time of the murder. At Stride's Inquest, the coroner, Mr Wynne Baxter, asked Dr Phillips about the wound and weapon used. In addition to a cut throat, 'was there', asked Baxter, 'any other similarity between this and Chapman's case?' Phillips was quite clear in his reply that:

> There is a great dissimilarity. In Chapman's case the neck was severed all round down to the vertebral column, the vertical bone being marked, and there had been an evident attempt to separate the bones.

The knife was also of a different kind to that used on Annie Chapman and Nichols. It was, according to Phillips, a rounded-end knife not a pointed one and could have been wielded by a right handed killer as opposed to the left handed individual who cut the throats of Nichols and Chapman. Furthermore, there were no mutilations whatsoever to Stride's body and unlike Nichols and Chapman she had not been strangled prior to her throat being cut. The argument that the killer would have inflicted mutilations if he had not been disturbed is not only an abuse of the facts but a wholly unsubstantiated leap of faith.

There was a fifteen minute gap between the attack on Stride at the entrance to Dutfield's Yard, as witnessed by Israel Schwartz at 12.45 p.m. and the discovery of her body by Louis Diemschutz' pony and trap at 1.00 a.m., which Ripperologists allege disturbed the killer. Dr Phillips told the Inquest that it would have taken two seconds to cut Stride's throat. If the killer had wanted to inflict

further mutilations, he would have had the best part of fifteen minutes to do so – clearly he did not.

In terms of odds and probability, it would seem a virtual impossibility that Stride would have been attacked twice in the space of fifteen minutes by two different assailants at exactly the same location. The individual seen by Schwartz was without doubt attacking Stride and was, to a high degree of certainty her murderer.

Catherine Eddowes' murder is again, contrary to myth, somewhat different to Nichols and Chapman. There were no signs of bruising, suggesting no strangulation. More profound were the mutilations. Her nose had been cut off and her face was extensively mutilated with cuts on her eye lids and an inverted V's cut under each eye. This kind of facial mutilation is common with killers who wish to depersonalise and dehumanise their victims. No facial mutilations of any kind were inflicted on Nichols, Chapman or Stride. Again, contrary to popular belief, the whole of Eddowes' uterus was not removed, only part of it. If we are to believe in a common killer who collects uteruses, what is the point of a partial uterus? On the other hand, her left kidney was removed in its entirety, which was not the case with any other victim. Photographs and autopsy diagrams also show that Eddowes entire chest was opened up.

The differences in the bodies of Catherine Eddowes and especially Mary Kelly make it hard to believe that they were killed by the same person who killed the other victims or even each other. The killer did not take Kelly's uterus.

The broad 'similarities' between the murdered women led the police (although not all of them) to assume at the time that the murders had all been done by the same person. Serial killers were unheard of at that time and the police were ill-equipped to deal with crimes of this nature. The coincidence of the timing, location and violence of the murders led to the natural assumption that one person had killed all the victims.

Most police forces now believe that murderers kill their victims in practically the same way every time (i.e., the Yorkshire Ripper, Fred and Rose West, Harold Shipman etc). This is patently not the case in this series of murders. To explain this away, the 'Escalation Theory' was adopted by some Ripperologists to account for the ratcheting up of violence in each case.

The conditions of Whitechapel made it surprisingly easy for murder to occur. The police were unable to do much to catch murderers at the time and police inability to catch the culprit(s) opens up the possibility that people began to realise that they too could get away with murder. There was enough panic in the streets, that any murder would be attributed to Jack the Ripper if the throat was violently slashed.

In spite of the terrible social conditions, murder itself was actually uncommon in Whitechapel in 1888 (although there was a good deal of petty violence). In 1887 for example, there were only eight reported murders in the whole of London. A series, or perceived series of murders, which invoked morbid fascination and was covered heavily and sensationally by the press, generated more murders. A murder rate far-above normal in the East End was to continue well into 1889 and 1890 as a result of these simple factors. Copycat murders involving slashed throats and/or abdominal mutilations were reported in the press as far away as Swansea.

If Superintendent Arnold, Dr Philips and Inspector Reid, to name but several individuals closely involved in the 1888 investigations were right, then the 'canonical five' theory, traceable back to Sir Melville Macnaghten, has to be seriously questioned, if not discarded, and the conclusion drawn that the Whitechapel murderer was not one man but several. If the task of identifying one killer has proven so problematic for over 120 years, one might assume that looking for more than one murderer would be a complete non-starter. Ironically, such an approach could actually have the opposite effect. For example, it would mean that each case could be assessed again and considered on its own evidence and individual merits, rather than trying to look for patterns and linkages with other cases that frankly might not exist.

From the very off, the Whitechapel investigation became swamped with successive layers of contaminated sediment, initially thrown up by press coverage. The relationship between press reporters and the police was very different then from today. In the 21st century, police investigations aim to actively work and liaise with the media. In 1888 there was no such realisation by the police of the benefits of working with the press nor indeed was there any desire to do so. Most police officers were especially suspicious of reporters and released very little to them. Of course, some reporters managed to obtain information by bribery, but on the whole a wall of enmity existed between police and press. Another profound difference was in the interviewing of witnesses by the press. There were not the restrictions that exist today and a sharp reporter might well manage to interview a victim's family members, neighbours and material witnesses before the police had even done so. In fact, it was not unusual for a witness, or more pertinently, someone claiming to be a witness, to have their story published in a newspaper before an official police interview had been conducted. The net result was that embellished, speculative and often contradictory accounts gained a foothold and later became an integral part of Ripper mythology.

Add to this the avalanche of Ripper letters that descended on the police and the successive waves of invented quotes, phoney evidence, fabrications and myths that were peddled by a number of authors during the following century, and we are left with a very murky pool indeed.

Sherlock Holmes author Sir Arthur Conan Doyle proffered on a number of occasions that the process of elimination was the most effective way to shed light on a conundrum. When you have progressively eliminated, piece by piece, the impossible and the improbable, whatever you have left is likely to lead towards an answer.

Is it then possible, after 120 years, to actually peel back these layers and reach the uncontaminated bedrock of evidence that might actually allow us to draw some realistic conclusions about the reality of these crimes?

CHAPTER 8

A PROCESS OF ELIMINATION

One of the most contaminated areas of evidence concerning the Whitechapel Murders concerns what was or was not observed by a range of witnesses who gave statements to the police. As noted in the previous chapter, it was not unusual in that era for hotfooted reporters to either get to witnesses (or those claiming to be witnesses) before the police, or to interview them after they had made police statements and induce a somewhat different version of events from them. Those writers who have sought in the past to produce books making the case for the guilt of their own chosen suspect, have often adopted the 'pick-and-mix' approach to such evidence, indiscriminately taking extracted morsels from police statements, press reports and other unverified sources alike.

In this way, one finds at first glance a canvass of evidence that seems to fit a particular suspect. However, when the origin of the various threads is studied in their overall context, a very artificial and somewhat prefabricated impression is gained. In respect to Mary Ann Nichols and Annie Chapman, for example, reality seems to indicate that no reliable eye witness testimony ever existed that could be of assistance to the police. Two days after the murder of Annie Chapman, the *Telegraph* claimed that:

At eight o'clock last night the Scotland Yard authorities had come to a definite conclusion as to the description of the murderer of two, at least, of the hapless women found dead at the East-end, and the following is the official telegram dispatched to every station throughout the metropolis and suburbs: "Commercial-street, 8.20 pm - Description of a man wanted, who entered a passage of the house at which the murder was committed with a prostitute, at 2.00 am on the 8th. Aged thirty-seven, height 5 ft 7 in, rather dark, beard and moustache; dress, short dark jacket, dark vest and trousers, black scarf and black felt hat; spoke with a foreign accent."

On 11 September *The Daily News* shed a little more light by reporting that the suspect had slipped into the passage of 'the house at which the murder was committed' with Emily Walton, a prostitute, also known as Emily Walters. Efforts to trace the existence of this woman have proved fruitless and the likelihood is that she never in fact existed. Indeed, her name is notable for its absence in Chief Inspector Swanson, review of the facts regarding the murder on 19 October 1888. In his report, he mentioned just a single witness, namely Elizabeth Long of Church Street, Whitechapel.

Long, apparently saw a man and woman talking on the pavement outside 29 Hanbury Street as she was walked along the street at 5.30 a.m. on 8 September. Her statement was taken seriously due to the discovery of Annie Chapman's body just thirty minutes later at the rear of the property. Long identified the body in the mortuary as being that of the woman she had seen earlier. He was apparently 'a little taller' than five feet in height, looked to be over forty and of a shabby genteel appearance. She believed him to be wearing a brown deerstalker hat and a dark overcoat.

Although his back was turned and she did not see his face, Long believed he was a foreigner, presumably from hearing his accent. The couple was apparently 'talking loudly' and she was able to overhear the man asking, 'Will you?' and the woman reply, 'Yes.' However, she had frequently seen couples 'standing there in the morning,' and so continued on her way, finding nothing suspicious about this particular pair.

Questions have been raised about the reliability of her statement, due to a reference in Chief Inspector Swanson's report of 19 October, in which he states that Dr Phillips:

> ... was called and saw the body at 6.20 am and then gives it as his opinion that death occurred about two hours earlier, viz: 4.20 am, hence the evidence of Mrs Long which appeared to be so important to the coroner, must be looked upon with some amount of doubt, which is to be regretted.

In fact, at the inquest on 19 September, the foreman of the jury had, 'remarked that the time stated by the witness (Elizabeth Long) was not consistent with that stated by the doctor.' The Coroner replied that, 'Dr Phillips had since qualified his statement.' In view of Phillip's qualification, Elizabeth Long's evidence may well be sound. However, we have no way of knowing whether her definition of a foreigner implied a Jew of eastern European origin, or an American, for example, or even a man from closer to home, i.e. an Irishman.

The morning of 30 September was marked by the so-called double event murders of Elizabeth Stride in Berner Street, and Catherine Eddowes in Mitre Square. Elizabeth Stride seems to have been seen with her murderer by a surprising number of witnesses. Again, these need to be carefully considered.

A PROCESS OF ELIMINATION

Elizabeth Stride was seen by two labourers, J. Best and J. Gardner, sheltering from the rain at 11.00 p.m. on the night of 29 September. They reported seeing her in the doorway of the Bricklayer's Arms on Settles Street, together with a man dressed in black morning suit and a billycock hat. They described him as having a black moustache, sandy eyelashes and being about 5 feet 5 inches tall.

Best reported that the couple, 'had been served in the public house and went out when me and my friends came in. It was raining very fast and they did not appear willing to go out. He was hugging and kissing her, and he seemed a respectably dressed man, we were rather astonished at the way he was going on with the woman.' They remarked to her 'Watch out, that's Leather Apron getting round you!' unable to resist a little light hearted banter at the couple's expense. However, at this they 'went off like a shot soon after 11', evidently mortified by the repartee. They scurried off towards Commercial Road, despite the continuing downpour, watched by Best and Gardner.

Best and Gardner made no statement to the police. Their recollections were given to an *Evening News* reporter two weeks later. It should also be noted that the behaviour of the man they saw seemed if anything to attract attention, hardly the behaviour of a killer who would not wish to be unduly noticed by future potential witnesses. The likelihood is that the couple they saw were not Stride and her killer, but another couple altogether.

Forty five minutes later, At 11.45 p.m., a man and woman were spotted outside 63 Berner Street by labourer William Marshall, standing outside his lodgings at number sixty-four. Apparently the couple seemed quite sober. They began to kiss, after which the man remarked to the woman, 'You would say anything but your prayers.' At this point, they walked towards Dutfield's Yard. The man was described by Marshall as having the appearance of a clerk, being middle aged and stout. He was respectably dressed, clean shaven and approximately 5 feet 6 inches tall. He was dressed in dark trousers, a small, black, cutaway coat and a round peaked cap.

Marshall gave the police a statement and at the inquest he admitted that, 'there was no lamp near and I did not see the face of the man she was talking to.' Marshall stated that he was standing at the door from, '11.30 p.m. to 12.' When asked by a member of the inquest jury whether or not it was raining at the time, he replied, 'No, it did not rain until nearly 3 o'clock.' While the couple described by Best and Gardner and by Marshall sound very similar, the discrepancy concerning the rain begs the question as to whether both sets of recollections relate to the same evening.

The most controversial 'recollection' of the night, however, relates to Matthew Packer, who lived two doors down from the International Working Men's Educational Club at 44 Berner Street, where he traded from his shuttered front window. While conducting door to door enquiries, Sergeant Stephen White called on Packer at 9.00 a.m. on 30 September. At this point, Packer was insistent that neither he nor his wife had seen anything unusual the previous night, and that he had shut his shop at 12.30 a.m. because of the rain. However, two days later he received a visit from two private detectives employed by the Whitechapel Vigilance Committee. Packer now seems to have experienced a recollection of lost memory, perhaps brought on by the mention of a reward being offered by the Vigilance Committee.

He now related how, at around 11.45 p.m. on the night of the murder, he had sold grapes to a couple from his shop window, and described the man as aged about thirty five, of stout square-build and about 5 feet 7 inches tall. He had a clerkly appearance, wearing a wide-awake hat and dark clothes. When interviewed about his story by the *Evening News* on 3 October, Packer suggested '…I am certain that he wasn't what I should call a working man or anything like us folks that live around here.'

According to his new account of events, the man had said, 'I say, old man, how do you sell your grapes?' to which Packer replied, 'Sixpence a pound the black 'uns, sir, and fourpence a pound the white 'uns.' At this, the man had asked the woman, 'Which will you have, my dear, black or white? You shall have whichever you like best.' The woman had chosen the black ones, after which the couple lingered in the street until 12.15 a.m., eating the grapes in the rain. They then stood listening to the singing in front of the Berner Street Club. Packer lost sight of them after that, as he had to shut up shop for the night.

To cap the lot, Packer claimed that the police 'haven't asked me a word about it yet … no policeman or detective has asked me a single question or come near my shop to find out if I knew anything about the grapes the murdered woman had been eating before her throat was cut.'

The very same day that Packer uttered these words to the reporter, Dr Phillips gave a report to the inquest that showed Elizabeth Stride had not eaten grapes before her murder. However, the *Evening News* was determined not to let the truth (let alone Dr Phillips) get in the way of a good story and duly printed the entire interview. So far as the murderer was concerned, the *Evening News* claimed that the Packer interview represented, 'the first real clue that has been obtained to his identity.' In reality, Packer's statement was a tissue of lies from beginning to end, motivated by the lure of the reward and encouraged by the private detectives who needed 'new evidence' to earn their fee. It is, however, still widely quoted today as received fact.

Just after 12.30 a.m., the time Packer claimed to have shut up his shop, PC William Smith observed a man and woman on the opposite side of the road to Dutfield's Yard, where Elizabeth Stride's body was later to be discovered at 1.00 a.m. His description is unsurprisingly somewhat different to Packer's. Although he described the man as being about five feet seven or eight inches tall, Smith's man had a dark complexion and was about twenty-eight years old. He was wearing dark clothing, a dark overcoat and a hard felt, deerstalker hat. Smith later identified the woman, who had a flower pinned to her jacket, as Elizabeth Stride. PC Smith had no reason to be suspicious of the couple, and so continued on his beat towards Commercial Road.

Bearing in mind that PC Smith saw Stride some ten to twenty minutes before her death, Chief Inspector Swanson understandably saw his statement as being of importance. In his report of 19 October, Swanson also identified the other key witness in the Stride murder, Israel Schwartz.

As noted in the previous chapter, at about 12.45 a.m. Schwartz observed a man walking ahead of him as he turned into Berner Street. The man paused at the gateway of Dutfield's Yard and started speaking to the woman standing there. When asked later who he thought the woman was, Schwartz was adamant that it had been Elizabeth Stride.

This made his statement vital to the investigation, although he gave all his evidence through an interpreter; being a Hungarian Jew and unable to speak any English. However, the interviews he later gave to journalists differed slightly in certain details from his original statement to the police, which is more than likely attributable to the use of a different translator and the tendency of the press to embellish such interviews.

On the Sunday evening Schwartz was interviewed by Inspector Abberline who considered his evidence to be sound and reliable. He described the man as aged about thirty, being approximately five feet five inches tall, with a full face and broad shoulders. His hair was dark, his complexion fair and he wore a small brown moustache. He seemed to Schwartz to be slightly intoxicated. He told Abberline that the man he saw:

> Tried to pull the woman into the street, but he turned her round & threw her down on the footway & the woman screamed three times, but not very loudly.

When the *Star* interviewed Schwartz earlier the same day, their translator produced a record that was used to write the following report:

> The Hungarian saw him put his hand on her shoulder and push her back into the passage, but, feeling rather timid of getting mixed up in quarrels, he crossed to the other side of the street.

This was the moment that a second man came out of the public house and lit a pipe. As Schwartz walked past this second man, the man attacking the woman shouted out across the street - 'Lipski!' It is a debatable point as to whether he was shouting at Schwartz or the man with the pipe. However, the significant point here is not who he was shouting at but the word he used. Israel Lipski was a Jewish immigrant who the previous year had poisoned Miriam

Angel, for which he was executed in August 1887. As Inspector Abberline makes clear in a report dated 1 November:

> The name has very frequently been used by persons as a mere ejaculation by way of endeavouring to insult the Jew to whom it has been addressed, and as Schwartz has a very strong Jewish appearance I am of the opinion it was addressed to him as he stopped to look at the man he saw apparently ill-using the deceased woman.

It can therefore be concluded that whoever the attacker was shouting at, he was using an anti-Semitic insult and was thus not himself a Jew. Schwartz, who took fright at the shout, ran off and by the time he reached the nearby railway arch, the other man was nowhere to be seen.

The second inference that could be taken from Schwartz' account relates to the fact that the man he describes apparently stopped, spoke to the woman, and attacked her within moments of doing so without any apparent precursor. This could suggest the victim and her attacker knew one another and this fracas related to an earlier argument or dispute between them.

Chief Inspector Swanson took the view that that although the physical descriptions given by PC Smith and Schwartz of Stride's companion were similar, there were, 'serious differences in description of dress', which made it unlikely that they were the same man. Some have questioned why Schwartz was not called to give evidence at the Inquest into Stride's death, inferring that this was because there was some doubt about his account. This is, yet again, a red-herring. Schwartz was not called in person as he was unable to speak or understand English. His evidence was able to be submitted in the form of his written statement.

The second murder in the early hours of 30 September is also significant in terms of witnesses and what they saw.

Harry Harris, Joseph Hyam Levy and Joseph Lawende, three Jewish gentlemen, left the Imperial Club on Duke Street, in the City of London, at 1.30 a.m. on 30 September. They noticed a man and woman talking together as they passed the junction of Duke Street and Church Passage, which led into Mitre Square. They could see that the woman's hand was resting on the man's chest, although she had her back to them. Levy declared brusquely to Harris, 'Look there, I don't like going home by myself when I see those characters about.' He was certain that the pair was up to no good, and hurried to get away. He therefore paid little attention to them, which rendered him unable to give a detailed description later. He did suggest, however, that the man may have been three inches or so taller than the woman.

Joseph Lawende was more observant:

I was at the Imperial Club together with Mr Joseph Levy and Mr Harry Harris. It was raining and we sat in the club till half-past one o'clock, when we left. I walked a little further from the others. Standing in the corner of Church Passage in Duke Street, which leads into Mitre Square, I saw a woman. She was standing with her face towards the man. I only saw her back. She had her hand on his chest. The man was taller than she was. He had a black jacket and black bonnet. I have seen the articles which it was stated belonged to her at the police station. My belief is that they were the same clothes which I had seen on the deceased. She appeared to me short. The man had a cloth cap on with a cloth peak. I have given a description of the man to the police. I doubt whether I should know him again.

The description Lawende made was not made public at the inquest and was only released by way of the *Police Gazette* on 19 October, under the headline of 'Apprehensions Sought':

> A man, age 30, height 5 ft 7 or 8 in, complexion fair, moustache fair, medium build; dress, pepper-and-salt colour loose jacket, grey cloth cap with peak of same material, reddish neckerchief tied in knot; appearance of a sailor.

Interestingly, the same edition of the *Gazette* carried the two Berner Street descriptions given by PC Smith and Israel Schwartz. Reading them consecutively, one is struck by the fact if the man who murdered Stride was the same as the man seen with Eddowes in Church Passage, he must have changed his collar and tie for a reddish neckerchief, his hard felt deerstalker hat for a peaked cap, his diagonal coat for a loose pepper-and-salt jacket, and changed his dark complexion for a light one.

As we shall see in due course, of all the witnesses the police interviewed throughout the Whitechapel investigations, Lawende was considered to be the person who had the best view of the killer, albeit for a few brief moments. Possibly due to Levy's remark about 'those characters', he took a closer look at the man and woman as he passed them by. Despite the poor light he was very close to the couple, no more than nine or ten feet away. This was a unique if brief opportunity, and when asked by Mr Crawford, the City Solicitor, watching the case on behalf of the police, 'would you know him again?' He stated that he would doubt it, which, as we shall see is somewhat different from being definitely unable to.

The most enigmatic of Whitechapel murder victims was perhaps

Mary Kelly who was apparently seen by witnesses a number of times in the hours before her death.

In her police statement of 9 November, Mary Anne Cox was described as 'a widow and an unfortunate,' this later term being a Victorian euphemism for prostitute. During the course of the night, Mary Ann made several journeys to the neighbouring streets from her lodging at 5 Miller's Court. It was on her return to Dorset Street between 11.45 p.m. and midnight, that she noticed Kelly walking ahead of her. She was accompanied by a man carrying a quart can of beer, and the two disappeared into Kelly's room just as Mary Anne turned into the court. She called out 'Good night Mary Jane,' the name by which she apparently knew Kelly, but heard only 'Good night' in reply. It appeared to her that Kelly was very drunk, and was having difficulty speaking. Cox described the man as about thirty-six years old, with side whiskers and a thick carroty moustache. He was approximately five feet five inches tall, with a fresh complexion and a blotchy face. His clothes were shabby, and included a black felt billycock hat and dark overcoat. When she left again just after midnight the light was on in Kelly's room and she heard her singing. When Cox returned again at 3.00 a.m. Kelly's room was dark and silent.

It would seem that her earlier client was not with her for long, as another witness, Sarah Lewis, a laundress, saw her around 2.30 a.m.

She had decided to spend the remainder of the night with a friend, Mrs Keyler. As she approached her lodging at 2 Miller's Court, she noticed a man on the opposite side of Dorset Street, standing against the lodging house. She described him as short and stout and wearing a black wideawake hat. The man standing in the street was looking up the court as if waiting for someone to come out. He was more than likely one George Hutchinson, whose witness statement has long been the source of controversy and debate.

Hutchinson only came forward as a witness on 12 November after the Kelly inquest had ended. He was interviewed by Inspector Abberline at Commercial Road police station;

> About 2 am 9th I was coming by Thrawl Street, Commercial Street, and just before I got to Flower and Dean Street I saw the murdered woman Kelly and she said to me Hutchinson will you lend me sixpence. I said I can't I have spent all my money going down Romford. She said good morning I must go and find some money. She went away towards Thrawl Street. A man coming in the opposite direction to Kelly tapped her on the shoulder and said something to her. They both burst out laughing. I heard her say alright to him and the man said you will be alright for what I have told you. He then placed his right hand around her shoulders.

Hutchinson went on to relate how he saw them go back to Miller's Court where he says he stood outside for forty-five minutes to see if they came out. He had returned from Romford too late to sleep at his usual lodging house, the Victoria Home in Commercial Street, and was clearly hoping to spend what remained of the night at Miller's court (he had known Kelly for three years, although it is unclear whether he was a friend or a client). When the couple did not re-appear, Hutchinson left at 3.00 a.m. and spent the rest the night on the streets. He gave an exceedingly good description of the man, indeed one which some modern Ripper writers have asserted to be too good:

Age about 34 or 35. Height 5ft 6 complexion pale, dark eyes and eye lashes, slight moustache, curled up each end, and hair dark, very surly looking dress long dark coat, collar and cuffs trimmed astracan and a dark jacket under. Light waistcoat dark trousers dark felt hat turned down in the middle. Button boots and gaiters with white buttons. Wore a very thick gold chain white lined collar. Black tie with horse pin. Respectable appearance walked very sharp. Jewish appearance. Can be identified.

This is by far the most detailed witness statement given to the police, but can hardly be considered 'too good', bearing in mind that Hutchinson had a particularly close and comparatively long look at the man. Although the essential physical description was somewhat basic in comparison to the description of the man's attire, it would not have been at all unnatural for Hutchinson's attention to have focused on what such a well-to-do man was wearing.

Further background to Hutchinson's statement can be found in an interview he gave to the Weekly Dispatch, published on 18 November, which is corroborated by Inspector Abberline's own report of 12 November. 'I believe that he lives in the neighbourhood', Hutchinson asserted, 'and I fancied that I saw him in Petticoat Lane on Sunday morning, although I am not sure … I have been looking for the man all day.' Abberline confirms in his report that he is satisfied that Hutchinson's statement is true and has detailed two officers to walk around the district with him, 'with a view to finding the man.'

It could well be that Hutchinson did, at a later date, see the man again, or that he was detained on the strength of the description.

Although not substantiated by any surviving police reports, we are told by the *Evening News* of 8 December that one Joseph Isaacs, a cigar maker resembling Hutchinson's description, had been arrested on 6 December, but was released within the day once he had been cleared of any involvement.

In due course the police clearly eliminated the description given by Hutchinson as that of the killer, who almost certainly met Kelly after 3.00 a.m. Due to the destruction of police notebooks and other everyday police paperwork, we will probably never know how this came about. However, this conclusion is clear from the statement of Sir Robert Anderson in his 1910 autobiography that the, 'only person who ever had a good view of the murderer ... was a Jew.' Hutchinson was not, of course a Jew, and Anderson's reference has always been assumed to be referring to Joseph Lawende.

This is further testified to by the fact that is was Lawende who was called on by the police in an attempt to identify James Sadler, the man suspected of murdering Francis Coles on the morning of 13 February 1891, as being responsible for the earlier murders. Although Lawende was unable to identify him, it is clear that initially the police believed that the Coles murder was the work of the Ripper and that in Sadler they might well have caught the man who had eluded them for over two years. While Sadler was eventually charged with Coles' murder, he was later discharged due to lack of evidence.

In summary then, we can conclude that of the five murders discussed in this chapter, only in the cases of Annie Chapman, Elizabeth Stride and Catherine Eddowes, are there reasonably reliable descriptions of the men seen with the respective victims, within short proximity of the time the murders occurred.

The man seen with Chapman does not match the other two descriptions and was most likely a foreigner. The murderer of Stride, apart from not fitting Elizabeth Long's description was not a Jew on account of the anti-Semitic insult he shouted across the street. As already noted above, there are several key differences between the man described by Schwartz and the man described by Lawende. Taken together with the profound differences in the way the two murders of 30 September were committed, it seems clear that these are two very different men.

We therefore appear to have three potential murderers and five murder victims. On the basis that it is already generally accepted that Emma Smith, Martha Tabram, Rose Mylett, Alice McKenzie and Francis Coles were murdered by others, we now have a theoretical possibility of up to eight murderers committing crimes in the Whitechapel district, within a comparatively short span of time.

This would not be the first time either, that a similar scenario and debate about serial murders has occurred. For example, the Boston Strangler murders in the United States, where thirteen extremely similar murders took place between 1962 and 1964 are a relevant case in point. In the year 2000, DNA testing proved that the individual assumed to be responsible for all the murders, Albert De Salvo, could not possibly have committed them all. A proportion of these were undoubtedly opportunist, copycat killings made to look like the Boston Strangler's modus operandi.

Although we are unable to utilise DNA in respect to the Whitechapel murders, could it be the case that medical evidence and opinion from 1888 could shed further light on the questions raised by the witness statements? Who were those, working behind the scenes, away from the limelight, with first hand knowledge of the medical evidence? Can they offer any retrospective help?

CHAPTER 9

THE MASK OF SANITY

In 1910 former Inspector Edmund Reid, who had been one of the key investigating officers in 1888, read stories in the newspapers about the impending publication of 'The Lighter Side of My Life', the autobiography of Sir Robert Anderson. In it Anderson claimed to know the identity of the Whitechapel killer and suggested that the police had known the killer's identity at the time of the murders, but had not been able to bring charges. A witness had, according to Anderson, apparently identified the killer but would not give evidence in court as he, like the murderer was a Jew. Reid was asked for his reaction to this statement by the *Morning Advertiser*. He told them:

> Now we have Sir Robert Anderson saying that 'Jack the Ripper' was a Jew. That I challenge him to prove; and what is more, it was never suggested at the time of the murders ... I challenge anyone to prove there was a tittle of evidence against any man.

Reid went on to say that:

> If Dr Bagster Phillips, who held the post-mortems in conjunction with Dr Percy Clark were still alive, he would confirm my

statement. Dr Clark, who resides in Spital Square, is still alive, and knows what I say is true.

Phillips, who had died of apoplexy on 27 October 1897, was described in his Lancet obituary, written by Clark, as 'a modest man who found self-advertising abhorrent ... under a brusque, quick manner engendered by his busy life, there was a warm, kind heart, and a large number of men and women of all classes are feeling that by his death they have lost a very real friend.'

Dr Phillips and Dr Clark were undoubtedly the ones best placed to have intimate inside knowledge of the individual murder cases and the medical characteristics of the crimes. Phillips, who had been the Police Surgeon for 'H' Division (Whitechapel) since 1865, had, despite his natural reserve, acquired a public profile. He was a well known character and someone whose activities were often reported in the press. Clark, as Phillips' assistant, lived in his shadow and was not at all well known, even after he took over Phillips' mantle in 1897. Despite his close involvement in the Whitechapel murder cases, his name is hardly ever to be found in the index of Ripper books.

Even more so than Phillips, Clark was an intensely private man. Apart from one rare interview published in the *East London Observer* on 14 May 1910, he was to keep his own counsel on the murders, the victims and the perpetrators. As a result of former Inspector Edmund Reid's statement about Anderson, he had been approached by a reporter from the *East London Observer* seeking verification of Reid's statement.

In answer to the question 'Do you think they were all the work of one man?' Clark replied:

I am not certain of that. You see, if you publish details of cases of that kind – and all the evidence at the inquests appeared in the papers – a weak minded individual will be induced to emulate the crime.

When pressed again, Clark said:

I think perhaps one man was responsible for three of them. I would not like to say he did the others.

Clark was also quoted as saying:

Dr Phillips did not believe in publishing details of these cases. The reporters never got the least information from him, so a great many of the details were pure imagination.

Phillips himself, unbeknown to the press, had expressed very similar views to those of Clark two decades earlier:

After careful & long consideration I cannot satisfy myself, on purely anatomical professional grounds that the perpetrator of all the 'Wh' Ch'l murders is one man. I am on the contrary impelled to a contrary conclusion. This noting the mode of procedure & the character of the mutilations & judging of motive in connection with the later.

Within twenty years of Dr Percy Clark's interview, the first Jack the Ripper film, Alfred Hitchcock's, *The Lodger*, was released in 1926 and the first Ripper book, *The Mystery of Jack the Ripper* by Leonard Matters was published in 1928.

When the Ripper industry finally took off, the views expressed by Phillips and Clark were not those that had a welcome or ready audience, if indeed any audience at all.

By the time the press took a renewed interest in any story, anecdote or theory about Jack the Ripper in the 1930s, Dr Clark had long since disappeared. Even the house he had inherited from Dr Phillips in 1897 at 2 Spital Square, Bishopsgate, had been demolished in 1928, and with it seemingly any last trace of Dr Percy Clark.

Born in 1864 in Ruckinge, Kent, Clark qualified as a surgeon in his early twenties and was admitted to the Royal College of Surgeons in 1884. Their membership records indicate his address at the time as being 22 Margaret Street, Cavendish Square, London.

Apparently Clark had kept papers, correspondence and photos concerning the major cases he had an involvement in, and showed some of these to the east London *Observer* reporter who called at Spital Square to conduct his one and only press interview in May 1910. What had become of this collection and more to the point, what had become of Percy Clark?

From past experience of trying to track and trace the movements of intentionally elusive characters such as Sidney Reilly, the so-called 'Ace of Spies', and William Melville, the original 'M' of the Secret Service, I had hoped that the unintentional elusiveness of Percy Clark might make for a more straightforward search. While this hope proved to be somewhat optimistic, ironically, the method that initially led to Reilly's international movements being uncovered also revealed the tracks of Dr Percy Clark.

The Board of Trade passenger lists of those passing through British ports between 1890 and 1960 produced the following entry:

Jack the Ripper

Name:	Dr Percy John Clark
Date of departure:	4 September 1925, London
Passenger destination port:	San Francisco, USA
Passenger destination:	San Francisco, USA
Date of Birth:	1864
Age:	61
Marital Status:	Married
Sex:	Male
Occupation:	Surgeon
Ship:	Lochgoil
Official Number:	146679
Master's Name:	W H Macey
Steamship Line:	Royal Mail Steam Packet Co
Other Passengers:	Mrs Eveline Clark, Miss Mary Clark

On arrival in San Francisco, Percy Clark, his wife and their twelve year old daughter were met by Percy's elder brother Harry who owned a fruit ranch and had been working for *Walt Disney Productions* in Hyperion in the Silver Lake district of Los Angeles.

Percy too bought a fruit ranch on Yosemite Highway, Merced. For a few years he prospered until he lost his land and consequently his money in the 'Olive Grove' scandal. Today, his granddaughter, Diane Marmion, remembers going to see the site of the ranch with her mother many years after it had passed out of the family's ownership. Aware of Dr Percy Clark's career as a police surgeon, his surviving family were most helpful in assisting with our re-assessment of the role he played in 1888.

At the time of the Whitechapel Murders, Percy Clark was not only a close confident of Dr George Bagster Phillips, but also of two distinguished neighbours, Sir James Risdon Bennett, a past President of the Royal College of Physicians, who lived at 22 Cavendish Square, and Dr George Savage, who lived on the opposite side of the square from Percy Clark, at 3 Henrietta Street. All three conferred on the murders and seem to have had markedly similar views, which Clark kept for posterity.

Professor Derrick Pounder, Head of Forensic Medicine at Dundee University and a senior government pathologist, played an invaluable role in the making of our Channel 5 documentary *Jack the Ripper: Tabloid Killer*. He had previously worked with me in 2004, reviewing the original Autopsy Report on the murder of Grigory Rasputin for *BBC Timewatch*, and I knew his views on the 1888 forensic evidence would add value to our 2009 analysis.

In reviewing the forensic evidence associated with the Whitechapel Murders for this book, Professor Pounder outlined his view that Phillips and Clark had indeed held back some of the evidence and detail relating to the mutilations and injuries at the inquests. Indeed, Clark so much as admitted this when he told the east London *Observer*, 'Dr Phillips did not believe in publishing details of these cases.' One is further reminded of the dialogue between Phillips and Coroner Mr Wynne Baxter at the Annie Chapman Inquest on 19 September 1888. On being recalled that day, Phillips was told by Baxter that all the evidence he had obtained from his post-mortem examination should be on the record of the court. Phillips retorted, that had notice been given to him he would have been better prepared, although he had his original notes with him. In other words, Phillips was happy to quote from his notes in court but not to divulge them in their entirety.

Phillips then proceeded to give his evidence. After only a short while, the coroner again interjected to point out to Phillips that; 'we are here to decide the cause of death, and therefore have a right to hear all particulars … I might add that I have never before heard of any evidence being kept back from the coroner.'

It is also worthy of note that the only full autopsy report that survives is that on Catherine Eddowes, which although Phillips and Clark were in attendance, was actually conducted by the surgeon of the City of London police, Dr Frederick Brown.

Shortly after the Stride and Eddowes murders, Sir James Risdon Bennett made the following observations:

> It must not too readily be assumed that the two murders of yesterday morning had the same object. Dr Phillips, who was called to Burner Street shortly after the discovery of the woman's body, gives it as his opinion that the two murders were not committed by the same man. Upon this point Dr Phillips is an authority.

> My impression is that the miscreant is a homicidal maniac. He has a specific delusion, and that delusion is erotic. Of course we have at this moment very little evidence indeed, in fact I may say no evidence at all, as to the state of the man's mind except so far as is suggested by the character of the injuries which he has inflicted upon his victims. I repeat that my impression is that he is suffering under an erotic delusion, but it may be that he is a religious fanatic. It is possible that he is labouring under the delusion that he has a mandate from the Almighty to purge the world of prostitutes, and in the prosecution of his mad theory he has determined upon a crusade against the unfortunates of

London, whom he seeks to mutilate by deprivation of the uterus. There are, on the other hand, a number of theories which might be speculated upon as to the particular form that his mania takes: but insomuch as we have no knowledge of the man himself, but only of the characteristics which surround the commission of his crimes wherewith to guide us, I come to the conclusion that his delusion has reference to matters of a sexual character.

A homicidal maniac, of the type described by Sir James Risdon Bennett appears absolutely normal; he will behave in what seems to be complete rationality, and nothing unusual will be noted about him. He will murder when the opportunity arises, and rarely bothers to dispose of the body, usually leaving it in the place in which the murder was committed. They typically perform whatever rituals they feel compelled to carry out, in this case mutilation, once the victim is dead.

According to Professor Derrick Pounder, the facial mutilations would be inflicted by the killer to depersonalise the victim and like the abdominal mutilations would be inflicted after cutting the throat. The killer had, as Professor Pounder observes:

> total control over the dead bodies, although they were still very warm and felt alive. The bowel would still be moving when he opened the abdomen, muscles would twitch when cut, and the blood was still warm and flowed freely.

Sir James Risdon Bennett goes on in his discourse to make further observations concerning coroner Wynne Baxter's observation about an American seeking an agent to procure uteruses:

Jack the Ripper

Even if it should transpire that in the case of the Mitre Square victim the uterus is missing, I should not be disposed to favour what I may call the American theory in the slightest degree, and I must confess that it was with considerable surprise that I noticed in certain newspapers a disposition to readily accept the theory which the coroner who investigated the circumstances attending the murder of the woman Chapman first suggested. It is my opinion that if any person wanted a number of specimens of the uterus, and was himself a man possessed of surgical skill, he would himself undertake to secure them rather than employ an agent. No love of gain could possibly induce a sane man to commit such atrocities as these, and besides this there is there is the circumstance remaining, as I have said, that they might all be secured at the medical institutions either of England or America. – that is to say if they were needed for legitimate purposes – practically without any consideration at all.

Bennett also touches on a matter of considerable relevance when he observes the following:

It has been said, and it is a very natural observation, that if the murderer were a lunatic he could not commit these crimes and escape with impunity. That is a comment which any person not fully acquainted with the peculiarities of lunatic subjects might very well make. In my view, however, the extraordinary cunning which is evinced by the homicide is a convincing proof of his insanity. No man could have escaped in just the same fashion as this man seems to have done. He must almost by necessity have betrayed himself. It is a matter of common knowledge, however, amongst doctors that lunatics display a wonderful intelligence.

It may be called so in their criminal operations, and I have little doubt that if the murderer were other than madman he would have been captured by the police.

Bennett's views are very much those that still hold true today. Professional opinion on 'asocial' psychopathic murders is that although they often have a below average IQ and rarely bother to cover their tracks, they may still evade capture for some time because of their innate level of cunning and risk taking. As Professor Pounder points out, 'taking organs with him carried a high risk if he was stopped and searched so this was clearly something important to him.'

An additional key point which Bennett returns to in conclusion is the issue of anatomical knowledge:

Dr Phillips has stated that the injuries inflicted upon these women have been apparently performed by a person possessing some anatomical knowledge. That is likely enough; but would not a butcher be quite capable of treating the body in this way?

Indeed, Clark, who no doubt shared and reflected Phillips' views, clarified the matter as follows:

One of the suppositions was that he (the killer) was a medical student or something of that sort. There was nothing of a professional character about these wounds. The bodies were simply slashed about from head to foot.

Professor Pounder, in reviewing the forensic evidence over a century later concurs with Clark:

I agree there is no suggestion of medical skill. The most impressive aspect of the cases is the infliction of the fatal throat wound with the victim lying down in situations which carry a high level of risk. This is someone who knows how to cut throats, possibly a slaughter-man.

The most persuasive evidence in terms of lack or indeed absence of medical skill is to be found in Dr Frederick Brown's autopsy report on Catherine Eddowes, which as noted earlier, was (unlike the Phillips/Clark autopsies) fully reported to the inquest.

Although Brown refers in his report to the killer having, 'some anatomical knowledge' he most certainly did not express the view that the killer had surgical knowledge. Essentially, Brown articulated the same view as Phillips, Clark and Sir James Risdon Bennett on this point. It has not, unfortunately, prevented a number of writers over the years from twisting 'some anatomical knowledge' to mean the same as surgical knowledge in order to fit their own theories. Brown's later observation that someone, 'in the habit of cutting up animals' would have had the necessary anatomical knowledge has often been deliberately ignored.

With regard to the left kidney, which forensic evidence suggests was removed before the uterus; Brown's observations indicate that this was very imprecisely done to say the least. A crude flap had been cut into the abdominal aorta and while the kidney is covered by the peritoneum membrane, Brown noted that this had probably been partly cut when the abdomen had been opened and the intestines removed. He also found that the area around the kidney had been subjected to random stabs, hardly an indication of precision and intention. Furthermore, in the process of attempting to remove the uterus, the killer unintentionally cut the lower end of the large bowel, namely the sigmoid colon, making the removal an even greater botch than has previously been appreciated. As a result of this accidental severing, the killer's hands would have become covered in faeces. This is a further reason for believing that the kidney was removed first; had it not been, there would undoubtedly have been faecal contamination caused by the killer's hand around the peritoneum, adjacent to the left kidney. Had this contamination been in evidence it would have been noted by Dr Brown and mentioned in the autopsy report, which it was not.

Although we do not have comparable data from the Phillips/Clark autopsy of Annie Chapman, due to Phillips' reluctance to divulge detail, it is clear from what we do have that there is a contrast in the way the uterus was removed from Annie Chapman and Catherine Eddowes. In the Chapman case, the uterus was removed with a clean precision cut below the cervix. Eddowes' uterus was removed by a clumsy incision above the cervix leaving a stump of the uterus behind. It was this cut that accidentally severed the sigmoid colon, a bend in the intestine that is virtually in line with the cervix.

It would also appear that as a result of this, the killer then moved to cut the upper part of the descending colon thus removing the intestine completely and placing it on the pavement to the left of the body. This would have further contaminated his hands with faeces and would explain why he then cut off part of Eddowes' apron with his knife in order to wipe his hands. This was later, of course, found in Goulston Street.

The only conclusion that one can possibly draw from Professor Pounder's observations, Dr Brown's autopsy and those carried out by Dr's Phillips and Clark, is that whoever the killer or killers were, they possessed nothing in the way of surgical skill, over and above a very basic awareness of where some organs were located. The methods used were, on the contrary, crude and haphazard, particularly so in the case of Catherine Eddowes.

The other friend and neighbour of Dr Clark's, Dr George Savage, clearly agreed with Phillips' approach on restricting information on the mutilations and was opposed to, 'the publicity which the press gives to the details of notorious crimes.' Also echoing the Phillips/Clark view on copycat killers, Savage ventured to make suggest that:

> The murders may not all have been committed by one man. There
> is a fashion in murders, or, rather, there are epidemics of similar
> crimes; or again, the imitative action may have come into play.

He also feels that the, 'cunning of the evasion, the ferocity of the crimes, the special selection of the victims, seem to me to depend either on a fiendishly criminal revenge, or else upon some fully organised delusion.' In this, he too seems to endorse the lunatic theory of expounded by Sir James Risdon Bennett.

When doctors in 1888 referred to 'lunatics', they were essentially describing someone with symptoms of cyclic mood disorders, a killer who was psychopathic rather than psychotic. Psychopaths lack empathy and guilt, are usually impulsive, do not conform to social or moral norms and often appear quite normal. Dr Hervey Cleckley, regarded by many as a pioneer in the field of psychopathy observed that, 'unlike people with major mental disorders, a psychopath can appear to be normal and even engaging, while typically not suffering overtly from hallucinations or delusions.' Cleckley's 1941 landmark study, *The Mask of Sanity* held as its central thesis that, 'the psychopath exhibits normal function according to standard psychotic criterion, yet privately engages in destructive behaviour.' The mask of sanity, according to Cleckley, effectively concealed the psychosis.

In reply to a question posed by the *East London Observer*, as to why, 'the police could get no clue' to solving the murders, Dr Percy Clark replied that, 'no one is more cunning than the maniac'. He went on to voice the view that, 'he would be one of the low type of which you see thousands loafing about the streets ...it is my idea that the perpetrator was a man who had become insane - probably a man of the lowest class ... I would say he was a man not in a descent position in life.

Professor Pounder also feels that to evade detection a killer would need to know, 'the area well, living or working there, be able to pass un-remarked on the streets, and take victims who probably approached him for money.' In this scenario he would have been an ordinary working man in employment, as to be otherwise would have meant it unlikely that his victims would have approached him in the expectation of money.

Behind a 'mask of sanity', such a killer would have hidden in plain view of everyone, an apparently ordinary and normal individual blending into the local community. Whitechapel had a number of slaughterhouses and butchers establishments. In an era before meat refrigeration, slaughterers and meat cutters had little time to slaughter animals and cut the meat while it was still fresh. Meat cutters therefore had to work quickly and precisely. We also know that during their investigations, the police made slaughterhouse employees a priority, with the full co-operation of the proprietors and managers of such establishments. According to a report in the *Star* on 4 October:

Every employee has been personally 'pumped'. Each man has been
called upon to give an account of himself and his whereabouts not
only on last Saturday night, but during the entire period over
which the series of crimes extends. Every peculiar circumstance is
made note of, and no one to whom the slightest suspicion attaches
is lost sight of until the suspicion is completely allayed. Nor has
the man's own word been accepted as conclusive. Each man has
been asked if he knows of any one who has not been regular at
his work or has played tricks on the timekeeper, for the time book
in each establishment plays an important part in the investigation.
More than all this, in some cases, all men who can write have
been called upon to make a statement in writing and sign their
names, so that any possible question of handwriting may be more
easily compared.

It is a strong possibility, that just as in the case of the Yorkshire
Ripper a century later, when Peter Sutcliffe was actually interviewed,
not once but several times by the police without connecting him to
the crime, an 1888 killer who worked in the slaughterhouses might
also have had the same experience.

Although we do not know which three victims Clark was
referring to when he said, 'I think perhaps one man was responsible
for three of them,' we are aware of Phillips' views on the, 'great
dissimilarity' in the case of Elizabeth Stride and the previous
victim, Annie Chapman. Coupled with the fact that his long time
friend Superintendent Thomas Arnold, head of the Whitechapel
police division, went on record in 1893 with the view that the
Miller's Court murder was not a Ripper killing, he could have been
referring to Nichols, Chapman and Eddowes. Whilst this is clearly
open to debate, one thing is undeniable:

Dr Phillips, Dr Clark, Sir James Risdon Bennett and Dr George Savage are all on record as asserting that the five so-called 'canonical' murders were not all committed by the same killer. Given that the victims prior and subsequent to the five murders were, by consensus, murdered by others, we therefore have a multi-murderer scenario whereby at least one was a homicidal psychopath.

Today, as in 1888, such killers are generally sent to Broadmoor. Originally founded in 1863 as the Broadmoor Asylum for the Criminally Insane, it is now a high security psychiatric hospital simply known as Broadmoor Hospital. In February 1894, a newly launched newspaper by the name of the *Sun* made a sensational allegation in a series of front page articles, claiming that the Whitechapel murderer was, 'In Broadmoor Criminal Lunatic Asylum.'

The man behind these dramatic claims was none other than Mr T.P. O'Connor, the *Sun's* founder and editor. Why had O'Connor left the *Star* and what would be the consequences of his renewed attempt to exploit the Jack the Ripper story?

CHAPTER 10

JOURNEY'S END

Within eighteen months of the Kelly murder, T.P. O'Connor found that his on-going conflict the *Star's* proprietors and directors was coming to a head. Clearly Brunner and Colman had decided that enough was enough. As previously noted, O'Connor had initially secured his position through the company's Articles of Association, thinking that this would ultimately protect him from any likely attempts to dispense with his services.

The commercial success of the *Star* had not stopped the proprietors from objecting to O'Connor's cavalier attitude, to the vulgarity of his approach to headlines and content and to his fulminations against the established order. It seems clear that key colleagues at the top of the *Star's* journalistic hierarchy had also, by this time, been recruited by the proprietors to assist in securing O'Connor's departure. In early 1890 confidential discussions began to sweeten the pill for O'Connor. Eventually after much soul searching, he agreed to resign his position as editor and director and to surrender his shares in the company in exchange for the sum of £15,000. Apparently he put most of this money into South African mining shares, which by 1914 had lost eighty per cent of their value.

Naturally, O'Connor saw the circumstances leading to his departure somewhat differently from Brunner and Colman, although his account is punctuated with occasion moments candour:

> The paper was going splendidly, its influence becoming daily
> greater. And just at this moment of omnipotence for my paper I
> began to have trouble-most of it, I now know, made by myself.
> For the first time I was in contact with a board of directors. I did
> not realise at the time anything about the laws which governed
> a concern under such control, and I really regarded it as purely
> nominal. Instead of consulting the directors as I should have done,
> and as I could have done, in most cases with perfect security of
> their accepting my views, I took action for myself. The first time
> on which I committed this stupid indiscretion was when, without
> consulting them, and in recognition of the splendid work he had
> done, I increased Mr. Massingham's salary by £10 a year. I gave to
> this member of my staff not merely unlimited confidence but also
> warm affection. But he was a bit worried at the time, as his first
> wife about to have a child. I protected him so far as I could from
> any great demand upon his time.

Although he never said so publicly, it was Massingham who was
to betray him to the proprietors in an arrangement that led to
Massingham himself being appointed editor in O'Connor's place.

> These things led to impatience on my part, and I was encouraged
> in that impatience by a member of my staff to whom I was foolish
> enough to listen. There came the first general meeting of the
> company. Everything was going all right until in an evil moment
> I let myself go, and began to speak critically of the interference of
> my directors.

Then came a blow which thoroughly paralyzed me. A man on the staff whom I regarded as my greatest and most faithful friend astounded me one day by sending out to the shareholders a printed indictment of me, full of misrepresentation and deadly in its venom.

The man who wrote and distributed the circular was Henry Massingham. It is highly unlikely he would have struck out at O'Connor in such a brazen and public way without some kind of advance understand that he would benefit from O'Connor's departure.

Of course I should treat such a manifesto, if it happened to-day, with contempt; but in these days of more sensitive and less experienced nerves it gave me a stab in the heart. I felt I had Judases all around me. Our board meetings became bear gardens. I had only one friend on the board, the late Mr. Wilfrid Blunt; but he was futile. And to make a long story short, I accepted an offer of fifteen thousand pounds for the purchase of my interest. What I wanted was respite from this continual strain on my nerves, and of course fifteen thousand pounds was a tempting sum after less than two years' work to a man who had not a penny when he started the paper.

Further light, in terms of the proprietors' the side of the story is shed by a letter John Brunner wrote to Massingham shortly after the deal to secure O'Connor's departure had been concluded. In fact, the only way the proprietors could find to untangle the web of defences O'Connor had woven into the 'Articles of Association' was to actually wind up the Newspaper Publishing Company Ltd and start afresh with the Star Newspaper Company Ltd.

Soon after the extraordinary general meeting of the Newspaper Publishing Ltd, Massingham was verbally offered the editorship of the *Star* and received this cursory letter from Brunner shortly before the offer was formally confirmed:

7 July 1890

Dear Sir.,

I have this afternoon received a memo from Mr. Stuart following the Extraordinary General Meeting of the Newspaper Publishing Company (Ltd) of 27th ultimo.

Mr Stuart advises that you would be agreeable to the proposals made by the company and we are most encouraged by your undertaking with respect to the standards expected of the newspaper. I have submitted on a number of occasions that Mr O'Connor's former use of compatriots such as Messrs. Best and O'Brien have not only been responsible for several potential legal actions against the Star, but in the unfortunate case of Mr Parke, a somewhat more serious consequence in January last.

Furthermore, Mr Best's attempt to mislead Central News during the Whitechapel Murders should have led to an earlier termination of his association with the newspaper.

I shall be glad to receive the favour of your reply, advising me of your intentions with regard to the other editorial matters previously discussed.

Jack the Ripper

Yours faithfully

John J Brunner, Esq., M.P.

The deal with O'Connor also involved a legally binding undertaking that he would not re-enter the newspaper industry for three years. O'Connor bided his time in Parliament during this hiatus, although as he later recalled in his memoirs:

> The thought of the return that had been made to me for all the labour I had given and all the success I had brought to the paper, and at the hands of those I considered my friends, worked on me by night and by day. I was bound not to start a paper in London for three years. I panted for that day when my freedom would be recovered; and I started a paper on that very day, called the Sun. I started it with insufficient capital; I found myself the Frankenstein of a monster which had so established itself from the original impulse I had given it that it could not be displaced.

When the time came to launch the new paper, O'Connor's mind must have recalled the person who, more than any other, had worked tirelessly to establish its foothold and to make it within months the largest selling evening paper in the country – Jack the Ripper. The *Sun* therefore launched with a five day front page serial story exclusively revealing that Jack the Ripper had been confined in Broadmoor since 1891. Although the man was not named, so much incidental information was given that the Metropolitan police knew O'Connor was referring to one Thomas Cutbush.

In fact, it was O'Connor's five day diatribe between 13 and 17 February 1894 that led to Sir Melville Macnaghten writing his now famous memo of 24 February 1894. Macnaghten opens his memo by stating:

> The case referred to in the sensational story told in 'the Sun' in its issue of 13th inst. & following dates, is that of Thomas Cutbush who was arraigned at the London County Sessions in April 1891 on a charge of maliciously wounding Florence Grace Johnson, and attempting to wound Isabella Fraser Anderson in Kennington. He was found to be insane, and sentenced to be detained during Her Majesty's Pleasure.

Macnaghten quite rightly alludes to the fact that Cutbush's antecedents hardly fitted with Jack the Ripper, a view born out by the release of his Broadmoor file on 18 November 2008. However, the five day serial certainly helped O'Connor launch his new paper with a bang.

He may not have exposed a killer, but then he was no more interested in who was responsible for the murders in 1894 than when he set the single maniac killer loose on the newspaper buying public six years previously. He was quite simply interested in one thing, selling papers.

Who the killers were is anyone's guess. Elizabeth Stride could well have been murdered by her abusive boyfriend Michael Kidney, against whom she brought assault charges the year before her murder. Mary Kelly too was rumoured to have been a possible victim of one of her lovers at the time, Joseph Barnett. James Sadler was charged with the murder of Frances Coles, but was released through lack of evidence. Without doubt a number of the murders were carried out by a psychopath whose identity was hidden behind a 'mask of sanity', others were copy cat killings.

Jack the Ripper

The last word should perhaps go to Dr Percy Clark. Despite his view that it was 'best to let the matter rest' he had this to say in his only ever press interview in 1910:

> 'As far as I heard, and I think I heard most about these cases, there was never the slightest clue to anybody … and it will remain so'

APPENDIX 1

STAR MAN INTERVIEWS

The 'Star Man' was an idea that according to O'Connor came from a young member of his staff. Essentially, the Star Man was a nameless reporter whose purpose in life was to scour the streets for news, opinions and background interviews. It is very likely that the Star Man was not necessarily one person, although it seems clear that the likes of Frederick Best and Michael O'Brian would have filled the Star Man's shoes during 1888. The following Star Man articles and interviews add an interesting dimension to the story of the Whitechapel murders.

A CLUE TO THE MURDERER

The only clue of any value thus far is furnished by Mrs. Fiddymont, wife of the proprietor of the Prince Albert public house, better known as the 'Clean House,' at the corner of Brushfield and Stewart Streets, half a mile from the scene of the murder. Mrs Fiddymont states that at seven o'clock this morning she was standing in the bar talking with another woman, a friend, in the first compartment. Suddenly there came into the middle compartment a man whose rough appearance frightened her. He had on a brown stiff hat, a dark coat and no waistcoat. He came in with his hat down over his eyes, and with his face partly concealed, asked for half a pint of four ale. She drew the ale, and meanwhile looked at him through the mirror at the back of the bar. As soon as he saw the woman in the other compartment watching him he turned his back, and got the partition between himself and her. The thing that struck Mrs Fiddymont particularly was the fact that there were blood spots on the back of his hand.

This, taken in conjunction with his appearance, caused her uneasiness. She also noticed that his shirt was torn. As soon as he had drunk the ale, which he swallowed at a gulp, he went out. Her friend went out also to watch him.

Her friend is Mrs. Mary Chappell, who lives at 28 Stewart Street, nearby. Her story corroborates Mrs Fiddymont's and is more particular When the man came in the expression of his eyes caught her attention, his look was so startling and terrifying. It frightened Mrs Fiddymont so that she requested her to stay. He wore a light blue check shirt, which was torn badly, into rags in fact, on the right shoulder. There was a narrow streak of blood under his right ear, parallel with the edge of his shirt. There was also dried blood between the fingers of his hand. When he went out she slipped out the other door, and watched him as he went towards Bishopsgate Street.

AT THE TEN BELLS

The proprietor of the Ten Bells is Mr E. Waldron. The house stands on the corner of Spitalfields Market, and opens early for the convenience of those who bring their goods from the country. One of the assistants gave some information to our reporter with reference to the rumour that the murdered woman was seen there this morning. He said: 'A woman did call in here about five o'clock. She was poorly dressed, having no bodice to her skirt. She was middle-aged. She just had something to drink, when a man called for her. He just popped his head in the door and retired immediately afterwards. He had on a little skull cap, and was, as far as I could see, without a coat. But he gave me no opportunity of seeing him. I think, however, I should know his face again, and I think I would also know the woman.' The description of the woman corresponds to a certain extent, especially with regard to age, hair, and clothing, with that of the victim of today.

AT THE LODGING HOUSE

Timothy Donovan, deputy at the lodging-house, 35 Dorset Street, interviewed by a *Star* reporter, said 'the woman came to the place at between half-past one and a quarter to two this morning the worse for drink - in fact, she was "very drunk." She went downstairs to the common kitchen, and when the deputy went down and asked for the money for her bed, she said she had not sufficient. She came upstairs and said, "Jim, I've been in the infirmary. I'm going out. I sha'n't be long." John Edwards, the watchman, went out after her and saw her go in the direction of Brushfield. Before she went to the lodging-house last night she had not been seen there since the Sunday before.

Last Saturday afternoon she came to the lodging-house with a man about 5ft. 6in., with a dark moustache and short beard, and dressed in the clothes of a laboring man. "He was not 'Leather Apron,' the deputy said. "Do you know him?" asked the *Star* man. "Yes, I ought to," was the answer; "I chucked him down the stairs; he tried to murder a woman here."

Coming back to the new horror, Donovan said the man who came to the place with the woman Sivvey on Saturday had come with her to the lodging-house every Saturday for the last six weeks. He used to stop with her at the lodging-house till Monday morning. The woman had spoken about him, and said he was a pensioner.

The other women in the lodging-house say that from what she had said at different times 'Dark Annie' was well connected. She used to do crochet work, and, from her conversation it was evident she was a woman of some education. Her husband seems to have been a soldier; but is now dead, and until lately the woman was in receipt of 10s. a week, which the other women supposed was a pension. But lately this allowance has been stopped, and since then she has been more frequently in want of money.

THE LEATHER APRON AND KNIFE

John Richardson, of 2 John Street, E.C., said to a *Star* reporter: - 'I am a porter in Spitalfields Market. I always go round to mother's (Mrs. Richardson, 29, Hanbury street) on market mornings just to see that everything is right in the back-yard, where her underground packing-case workshops are. The place was burgled a short time back. This morning, as near as I know, it was ten minutes to five o'clock when I entered the backyard of twenty-nine. There was nobody there. Of that I am sure. I heard in the market at 6.20 a.m. a woman had been found murdered at mother's, and went round and saw the body. The police, by the doctor's order, took possession on my leather apron and knife that were on the premises, and also a box of nails, as well as three pills found near the body'.

THE MAN WHO FOUND THE BODY INTERVIEWED

The first to find the body was Mr. Diemshitz, steward of the club. Interviewed by a *Star* reporter, Mr. Diemshitz said: 'I was coming home from market at one o'clock on Sunday morning. I am a traveller by trade, and go to different markets to sell my goods. Yesterday I went to Westow-hill. As the night was so wet I did not stay quite so late as usual. After I had passed through the gate which had been left open on driving into the yard my donkey shied a little in consequence of my cart coming in contact with something on the ground. On looking down I saw the ground was not level, so I took the butt end of my whip and touched what appeared to me in the dark to be a heap of dirt lately placed there, a thing I was not accustomed to see. Not being able to move it, I struck a match and found it was a woman.

First of all I thought it was my wife, but I found her inside the club enjoying herself with the others. I said to some of the members there is a woman lying in the yard, and I think she is drunk. Young Isaacs, a tailor machinist, went to the door and struck a match, and to our horror we saw blood trickling down the gutter almost from the gate to the club. The dance was immediately stopped. I and Isaacs ran out for a policeman, but could not find one after traversing several streets, but in the meantime another man from the Club, Eagle, ran to the Leman-street police-station and fetched two policemen, who arrived about seven minutes after the discovery'.

THE SECOND TRAGEDY

Police constable Watkins, the man in question, was on duty there, and no more conscientious officer is in the force. His inspector speaks of him in the highest terms. He was on duty on the same beat last night, and a *Star* man went carefully over the same ground covered by him on the preceding night. 'I was working left-handed last night,' said the police officer. 'Sometimes I go into

Mitre-square through the Church-passage, but last night I entered from Mitre-street. It was just half-past one when I turned out of Aldgate and passed round the next corner into the square. At that time there was nothing unusual to be seen. I looked carefully in all the corners, as I always do, turning my lantern light in every direction. I am positive there was nothing wrong at that time.'

'And when did you pass through the square again?' asked the reporter.

'At about a quarter before two.'

'Had you met any person on your rounds?'

'Not a soul.'

'Nor heard any noise?'

'Not a sound, but the echo of my own footsteps.'

'You entered the square the same way?'

'Just the same. Here we are now at the entrance to the square. I came this way, stopped at this corner to look up and down the street, and then turned in. As I came to the back of this picture frame maker's I turned my light into the corner, and there lay the woman.'

'Did you recognise the situation at once?'

'Well, I can tell you it didn't take me a moment to see that the Whitechapel murderer had been our way. Her head lay here on this coal-hole,' said he, throwing the light of his lantern on it, 'and her clothes were thrown up breast-high. But the first thing I noticed was that she was ripped up like a pig in the market. There was the big gash up the stomach, the entrails torn out and flung in a heap about her neck; some of them appeared to be lying in the ugly cut at the throat, and the face - well, there was no face. Anyone who knew the woman alive would never recognise her by her face. I have been in the force a long while, but I never saw such a sight. I went at once to Dr. Sequeira and some of the others rushed off to the station house.'

'Were there any signs of a struggle?'

'None at all. There was perhaps a quart of blood on the stones, but there were no footprints or finger marks, except where the woman's chemise had been caught hold of as if it had fallen down in the way. Her clothing was filthy.'

THE NIGHT WATCHMAN'S STORY

The 'Star Man' next got hold of Morris, the watchman at Kearley and Tonge's. He was standing at the door, and said, first, that he had just been through the warehouse and had gone to the front door to look out into the square two moments before Watkins called to him last night.

'Do you always take a look out into the square?'

'Every night in the week, barring Saturday night, I stand at this door and smoke my pipe from one till two o'clock. It is a habit with me, and the police on the beat know it well, but on Saturday nights I have some work to do inside that interferes with it.'

'Did you see anything lying about that indicated what sort of man the murderer might be?'

'I saw the doctor pick up two studs out of the pool of blood and put them in the shell.'

'But are there any signs of a struggle having taken place?'

'No, but the studs might have been worked out by the man's own exertions in using the knife.'

PC PEARCE

PC Pearce, who lives at No. 3, opposite where the body was found, slept the while calmly, and his wife shared both his bed and his composure. She had left a light burning in the first floor front, and the blind was halfway up, a fact that could hardly have escaped the notice of anyone entering the square. 'I only wish it had been my luck to have dropped on that chap,' was the way Pearce put it to the 'Star Man,' but, to tell you the truth, I knew nothing about it till I was waked up this morning.' Just through the north-east passage is the fire brigade station, and none of those on duty saw or heard anything unusual, so quietly was the deed committed, and so carefully did the man make his exit.

THE DOCTOR

One of the doctors in an interview with a *Star* reporter, after describing the various wounds, said the woman belonged to the very poorest class. She appeared to be an outcast, and carried her tea and sugar about with her. She was very thin. 'I should say, from the fact that her hands were brown, that she had just come from the country - had been hop picking, perhaps. I think she was an Irish woman.'

'Does the form of her features make you think so?'

'No, but because she carried a pipe. The woman's throat,' continued the doctor, 'had first been cut, and it had been cut while the woman was on the ground. How do I know that? Because there was no blood in front.'

'Do you think that the murderer was a skilled man?'

'He had some knowledge of how to use a knife. The knife which he used must have been very sharp.'

'How long would it have taken him to mutilate the body as you found it?'

'At least five minutes.'

A *Star* reporter saw Dr J.G. Sequiera, 34, Jewry Street, who was the first medical man on the spot. 'I was there,' he said, 'about 10 minutes after the policeman found the body. The woman could not have been dead more than a quarter of an hour. The work had been quickly done.'

'By an expert, do you think?'

'No, not by an expert, but by a man who was not altogether ignorant of the use of the knife. It would have taken about three minutes.'

THE MUFFLED INDIVIDUAL

If the 'Star Man' had been in search of gore instead of news he need not have feared molestation as he went on to Duke-street. There was not even a policeman in sight, notwithstanding the extra force. When he had turned down through Church Passage into the square, however, he found four. He recalled the old proverb about locking the barn after the horse had been stolen. Certainly the red-hand would get a warm grip if it was stretched out there again this morning. It was now just five-and-twenty minutes of two. There were six people in the square all told, but no-one was making any noise. Presently footsteps were heard coming along the narrow passage leading from the other square, and when the newcomers appeared, their blue jackets and white aprons discovered their calling at once, and one could not escape the thought that here was evidence that slaughters were not strangers to Mitre-square. Then arose a train of reasoning that might have led back to the *Star's* original theory of a slaughterman having to do with some of the earlier murders, but just then the crescent moon sailed up above the surrounding buildings, and the 'Star Man' resigned into her hands the duty of throwing light upon the mystery of the dark corner.

Thomas Bates, a watchman, told a reporter that 'Long Liz' had lived with them for five or six years, but her real name he never knew. She was a Swede by birth. Her husband was shipwrecked and drowned. She was a clean and hardworking woman. Her usual occupation was that of a charwoman, and it was only when driven to extremities that she walked the streets. She would at times disappear for a month or so – even for as much as three months. She returned to the house on Tuesday last, after a prolonged absence, and remained there until Saturday night. That evening she went out about seven o'clock, and she appeared to be in cheery spirits. The fact of her not returning that night was not taken any particular notice of. Their apprehensions, however, were aroused when rumours of the murders reached them. While narrating these facts the watchman was affected, and wound up his statement by exclaiming, 'Lor' bless you, when she could get no work she had to do the best she could for her living, but a neater and a cleaner woman never lived.'

THE SIMPLE STORY OF HER "MATE"

The man's name is John Kelly, and is one of very great interest, throwing no light on the probable authorship of the crime, but illustrating in a very pathetic manner the mode of life in those low lodging houses. A *Star* reporter had a long conversation with Kelly this morning at the lodging house, No. 55, Flower and Dean street. He is about forty years of age, and, to all appearance, is a poor hard-working man. He told his story in a manner that carried with it an unmistakable stamp of genuineness. At times he almost broke down with emotion, for, as he expressed it, 'I have lived with that girl a long while, and we never quarrelled.' We will give his story as nearly as possible in his own words:

'It is nigh on to seven years since I met Kate, and it was in this very lodging-house I first set eyes on her. We got throwed together a good bit, and the result was that we made a regular bargain. We have lived here ever since, as the people here will tell you, and have never left here except when we've gone to the country together hopping. I don't pretend that she was my wife. She was not. She told me long ago that she had a husband, and told me what his name was. It was Tom Conway. She said he was a pensioner from the Royal Irish Artillery. She had had several children by him, but I don't know that I ever heard where they were except one daughter, who is married to a gunmaker and lives in King-street, Bermondsey. She told me all about her husband one night, when I spoke about the letters "T. C." being pricked in her arm. It was Conway that did that years and years ago, and it was by them letters partly that I recognised her last night. But she had a falling out with her husband and they parted.

She used to tell me she never wanted to see him again, but I remember her saying once or twice that she had met him in the street. The last time she spoke of him was a good while ago. She never said anything about his trying to cause her any trouble, or that she was in any way afraid of him. I don't believe he ever bothered her at all. Well, Kate and me lived on here as best we could. She got a job of charring now an then, and I picked up all the odd jobs I could in the Spitalfields Market. The people here were very kind to us. If Kate ever went with other men I never knew it. She would take a drop to drink, but she was never troublesome. I remember once she was up at the police station, and I suppose the police officers were right who thought they recognised her by that. We went hopping together mostly every year. We went down this year as usual. We didn't get on any too well, and started to hoof it home. We came along in company with another man and woman who had worked in the same fields, but who parted with us to go to Chatham when we turned off towards Maidstone. The woman said to Kate, "I have got for a flannel shirt. I wish you'd take it, since you're going up to town. It is only in for 9d., and it may fit your old man". So Kate took it and we trudged along. It was in at Jones's, Church-street, in the name of Emily Burrell. She put the ticket back in our box and we moved on. We did not have money enough to keep us going till we got to town, but we did get there and came straight to this house. Luck was dead against us. On last Saturday morning we were both done up for cash. I had nothing but a pair of boots that would bring anything, and I says to her, "We'll pop the boots and have a bite to eat anyway." "Oh, no," says she, "don't do that;" but I told her I'd pawn the shirt off my back to keep her out of the street, for she had had only a few odd jobs for a goodish spell back but she said she'd go and see what her daughter could do. We sat in this 'ere kitchen and had what turned out to be our last meal together.

She told me she had made up her mind to go to her daughter's in Bermondsey. I begged her to be back early, for we had been talking about the Whitechapel murders, and I said I did not want to have that knife get at her. "Don't you fear for me," said she, "I'll take care of myself, and I shan't fall into his hands." With that she went out. I went with her to the street corner below, and I never laid eyes on her again till I saw her down at the mortuary last night. I was out in the market all day, but did no good. When she did not come home at night I didn't worry, for I thought her daughter might have asked her to stay over Sunday with her.

So on Sunday morning I wandered round in the crowds that had been gathered by the talk about the two fresh murders. I stood and looked at the very spot where my poor old gal had laid with her body all cut to pieces and I never knew it. I never thought of her in connection with it, for I thought she was safe at her daughter's. Yesterday morning I began to be worried a bit, but I did not guess the truth until after I had come back from another bad day in the market. I came in here and asked for Kate, she had not been in. I sat down on that bench by the table and carelessly picked up a *Star* paper. I read down the page a bit, and my eye caught the name of 'Burrill'. It looked familiar, but I didn't think where I had seen it until I came to the word "pawn-ticket." Then it came over me all at once. The tin box, the two pawn-tickets, the one for that flannel shirt, and the other for my boots. But could Kate have lost them? I read a little further. "The woman had the letters 'T. C.,' in India ink, on her arm." Man, you could have knocked me down with a feather. It was my Kate, and no other. I don't know how I braced up to go to the police, but I did. They took me down to see the body, and I knew it was her.

I knew it before I saw it, and I knew her for all the way she was cut. I told the police all I have told you, and I suppose I will tell it again to the Coroner. I never knew if she went to her daughters at all. I only wish to God she had, for we had lived together a long while and never had a quarrel.'

JOE BARNETT'S STORY

In a public-house close by Buller's the reporter succeded later on in finding Barnett, who is an Irishman by parentage and a Londoner by birth. He had lived with her for a year and a half, he said, and should not have left her except for her violent habits.

Jack the Ripper

She was a Limerick woman by birth, he says, but had lived in Dublin for some time. She went by the name of Mary Jane, but her real name was Marie Jeanette. He knew nothing about her proceedings since he left her, except that his brother met her on the Thursday evening and spoke to her. He himself had been taken by the police down to Dorset-street, and had been kept there for two hours and a half. He saw the body by peeping through the window.

To our reporter Barnett said he and the deceased were very happy and comfortable together until another woman came to sleep in their room, to which he strongly objected. Finally, after the woman had been there two or three nights he quarrelled with the woman whom he called his wife and left her. The next day, however, he returned and gave Kelly some money. He called several other days and gave her money when he had it. On Thursday night he visited her between half-past seven and eight, and told her he was sorry he had no money to give her. He saw nothing more of her. She used to occasionally go to the Elephant and Castle district to visit a friend who was in the same position of life as herself. Kelly had a little boy, aged about six or seven years, living with her.

LAST SEEN ALIVE

There are conflicting statements as to when the woman was last seen alive, but that upon which most reliance appears to be placed, is that of a young woman, an associate of the deceased, who states that about half-past ten o'clock on Thursday night she met the murdered woman at the corner of Dorset-street, who said to her that she had no money and, if she could not get any, would never go out any more, but would do away with herself. Soon afterwards they parted, and a man, respectably dressed came up and spoke to the murdered woman Kelly and offered her some money. The man then accompanied the woman home to her lodgings, and the little boy was removed from the room and taken to a neighbour's house. About one o'clock in the morning a person living in the court opposite to the room occupied by the murdered woman heard her singing the song, "Sweet violets," but this person is unable to say whether anyone else was with her at that time. Nothing more was seen of the woman until yesterday morning, when, it is stated the little boy was sent back into the house, and, the report goes, he was sent out subsequently on an errand by the man who was in the house with his mother. There is no direct confirmation of this statement. A tailor named Lewis says he saw Kelly come out about eight o'clock yesterday morning and go back. Another statement is to the effect that Kelly was seen in a public-house known as the Ringers, at the corner of Dorset-street and Commercial-street, about ten o'clock yesterday morning, and that she there met her lover Barnett, and had a glass of beer with him. This statement also is not substantiated.

Sarah Roney, a girl about 20 years of age, states that she was with two other girls on Thursday night in Brushfield-street, which is near Dorset-street, when a man wearing a tall hat and a black coat, and carrying a black bag, came up to her and said, 'Will you come with me?' She told him she would not, and asked him what he had in the bag, and he said, 'Something the ladies don't like.' He then walked away.

A NEIGHBOUR'S DOUBTFUL STORY

Jack the Ripper

A woman named Kennedy was on the night of the murder staying with her parents at a house situate in the court immediately opposite the room in which the body of Mary Kelly was found. This woman's statement, if true, establishes the time at which the murderer commenced his operations upon his victim. She states that about three o'clock on Friday morning she entered Dorset-street on her way to her parent's house, which is situated immediately opposite that in which the murder was committed. She noticed three persons at the corner of the street near the Britannia public house. There was a man - a young man, respectably dressed, and with a dark moustache - talking to a woman whom she did not know, and also a female poorly clad, and without any headgear. The man and woman appeared to be the worse for liquor, and she heard the man ask, 'Are you coming.' Whereupon the woman, who appeared to be obstinate, turned in an opposite direction to which the man apparently wished her to go. Mrs. Kennedy went on her way and nothing unusual occurred until about half an hour later. She states that she did not retire to rest immediately after she reached her parents' abode, but sat up, and between half-past three and a quarter to four she heard a cry of 'Murder' in a woman's voice proceed from the direction in which Mary Kelly's room was situated. As the cry was not repeated she took no further notice of the circumstance until this morning, when she found the police in possession of the place, preventing all egress to the occupants of the small houses in this court. When questioned by the police as to what she had heard throughout the night, she made a statement to the above effect.

THE AUTOPSIES

Emma Smith

The post mortem was carried out by Dr G.H. Hillier, house surgeon at the London Hospital. Dr Hillier was on duty when the deceased was brought into the hospital by Mary Russell, deputy-keeper of a common lodging house in George Street Spitalfields. She had been attacked by two or three men who robbed her of money.

Dr Hillier reported the following at the inquest on 7 April:

> The injuries which the woman had received were horrible. A portion of the right ear was torn and there was a rupture of the peritoneum and other internal organs caused by some blunt instrument. It had penetrated the peritoneum, producing peritonitis, which was undoubtedly the cause of death. The woman appeared to know what she was about, but she had probably had some drink. The organs were generally normal. I have no doubt that death was caused by the perineum, the abdomen, and the peritoneum. Great force must have been used. The injuries had set up peritonitis, which resulted in death on the following day after admission.

Martha Tabram

The post mortem was carried out by Dr T.R. Killeen of 68 Brick Lane who also examined the body at the murder scene. Dr Killeen reported the following to the inquest on 9 August:

> I was called to the deceased, and found her dead. She had 39 stabs on the body. She had been dead some 3 hours. Her age was about 36, and the body was very well nourished.

> The left lung was penetrated in five places, and the right lung penetrated in two places. The heart, which was rather fatty, was penetrated in one place, and that would be sufficient to cause death. The liver was healthy, but was penetrated in five places, the spleen was penetrated in two places, and the stomach, which was perfectly healthy was penetrated in six places. I do not think all the wounds were inflicted with the same instrument. The wounds generally might have been inflicted by a knife, but such an instrument could not have inflicted one of the wounds, which went through the chest bone. My opinion is that one of the wounds was inflicted by some kind of dagger, and that all of them were caused during life.

Mary Ann Nichols

The post mortem was carried out by Dr Henry Llewellyn, of 152 Whitechapel Road, who also examined the body at the murder scene. Dr Llewellyn reported the following to the inquest on 3 September:

Five teeth were missing, and there was a slight laceration of the tongue. There was a bruise running along the lower part of the jaw on the right side of the face. That might have been caused by a blow from a fist or pressure from a thumb. There was a circular bruise on the left side of the face which also might have been inflicted by the pressure of the fingers. On the left side of the neck, about 1 inch in front of it, was a circular incision, which terminated at a point about 3 inches below the right jaw. That incision completely severed all the tissues down to the vertebrae. The large vessels of the neck on both sides were severed. The incision was about 8 inches in length. The cuts must have been caused by a long bladed knife, moderately sharp, and used with great violence. No blood was found on the breast, either on the body or on the clothes. There were no injuries about the body until just about the lower part of the abdomen. Two or three inches from the left side was a wound running in a jagged manner. The wound was a very deep one, and the tissues were cut through. There were several incisions running across the abdomen. There were three or four similar cuts running downwards, on the right side, all of which had been caused by a knife which had been used violently up and downwards, the injuries were from left to right and might have been done by a left handed person. All the injuries had been caused by the same instrument.

Annie Chapman

The post mortem was carried out by Dr George Bagster Phillips of 2 Spital Square, a police divisional surgeon, who also examined the body at the murder scene. Dr Phillips reported the following to the inquest on 13 September:

Jack the Ripper

There was a protusion of the tongue and a bruise over the right temple. On the upper eyelid there was a bruise, and there were two distinct bruises, each the size of a man's thumb, on the forepart of the top of the chest. The stiffness of the limbs was now well marked. There was a bruise over the middle part of the bone of the right hand. There was an old scar of the left of the frontal bone. The stiffness was more noticeable on the left side, especially in the fingers, which were partly closed. There was an abrasion over the ring finger, with distinct markings of a ring or rings. The throat had been severed as before describes. The incisions into the skin indicated that they had been made from the left side of the neck. There were two distinct clean cuts on the left side of the spine. There were parallel with each other and separated by about half an inch. The muscular structures appeared as though an attempt had made to separate the bones of the neck. There were various other mutilations of the body, but he was of the opinion that they occurred subsequent to the death of the woman, and to the large escape of blood from the division of the neck.

The deceased was far advanced in disease of the lungs and membranes of the brain, but they had nothing to do with the cause of death. The stomach contained little food, but there was not any sign of fluid. There was no appearance of the deceased having taken alcohol, but there were signs of great deprivation and he should say she had been badly fed. He was convinced she had not taken any strong alcohol for some hours before her death. The injuries were certainly not self-inflicted. The bruises on the face were evidently recent, especially about the chin and side of the jaw, but the bruises in front of the chest and temple were of longer standing – probably of days. He was of the opinion that the person who cut the deceased throat took hold of her by the chin, and then commenced the incision from left to right. He thought it was highly probable that a person could call out, but with regard to an idea that she might have been gagged he could only point to the swollen face and the protruding tongue, both of which were signs of suffocation.

The abdomen had been entirely laid open: the intestines, severed from their mesenteric attachments, had been lifted out the body and placed on the shoulder of the corpse; whilst the pelvis, the uterus and its appendages with the upper portion of the vagina and the posterior two thirds of the bladder, had been entirely removed. No trace of these parts could be found and the incisions were cleanly cut, avoiding the rectum, and dividing the vagina low enough to avoid injury to the cervix uteri. Obviously the work was that of an expert – of one, at least, who had such knowledge of anatomical or pathological examinations as to be enabled to secure the pelvic organs with one sweep of the knife, which must therefore have at least 5 or 6 inches in length, probably more. The appearance of the cuts confirmed him in the opinion that the instrument, like the one which divided the neck, had been of a very sharp character. The mode in which the knife had been used seemed to indicate great anatomical knowledge.

Elizabeth Stride

The post mortem was carried out by Dr George Bagster Phillips who reported the following to the inquest on 3 October:

Rigor mortis was still thoroughly marked. There was mud on the left side of the face and it was matted in the head.

The body was fairly nourished. Over both shoulders, especially the right, and under the collarbone and in front of the chest there was a bluish discoloration, which I have watched and have seen on two occasions since.

There was a clear cut incision in the neck. It was six inches in length and commenced two and a half inches in a straight line below the angle of the jaw, one half inch in over an undivided muscle, and then becoming deeper, dividing the sheath. The cut was very clean and deviated a little downwards. The arteries and other vessels contained in the sheath were all cut through.

The cut through the tissues on the right side was more superficial, and tailed off to about two inches below the right angle of the jaw. The deep vessels on that side were uninjured. From this it was evident that the haemorrhage was caused through the partial severance of the left carotid artery.

Decomposition had commenced on the skin. Dark brown spots were on the anterior surface of the left chin. There was a deformity in the bones of the right leg, which was not straight, but bowed forwards. There was no recent external injury, save to the neck. The body being washed more thoroughly I could see some healing sores. The lobe of the left ear was torn as if removal or wearing through of an earring, but it was thoroughly healed. On removing the scalp there was no sign of extravasation of blood.

Catherine Eddowes

This murder was the only one committed outside the Metropolitan

Police boundary in the City of London police district. Therefore, Dr Frederick Brown of 17 Finsbury Circus, surgeon of the City of London police force examined the body at the murder scene along with Dr George Sequeira of 34 Jewry Lane, Aldgate. Dr Brown carried out the post mortem (which is the only post-mortem report to have survived in its entirety) and reported as follows to the inquest held on 4 October:

> I made a post mortem examination at half past two on Sunday afternoon. Rigor mortis was well marked; body not quite cold. Green discoloration over the abdomen. After washing the left hand carefully, a bruise the size of a sixpence, recent and red, was discovered on the back of the left hand between the thumb and first finger. A few small bruises on right shin of older date. The hands and arms were bronzed. No bruises on the scalp, the back, body or elbows.
>
> The face was very much mutilated. There was a cut about a quarter of an inch through the lower left eyelid, dividing the structures completely through. The upper eyelid on that side, there was a scratch through the skin of the left upper eyelid, near to the angle of the nose. The right eyelid was cut through to about half an inch.
>
> There was a deep cut over the bridge of the nose, extending from the left border of the nasal bone down near the angle of the jaw on the right side of the cheek. This cut went into the bone and divided all the structures of the cheek except the mucous membrane of the mouth. The tip of the nose was quite detached by another oblique cut. There was a cut on the right angle of the mouth as if the cut of a point of a knife. The cut extended an inch and a half, parallel with the lower lip.

Jack the Ripper

There was on each side of cheek a cut which peeled up the skin, forming a triangular flap about an inch and a half. On the left cheek there were two abrasions of the epithelium under the left ear. The throat was cut across to the extent of about six or seven inches. A superficial cut commenced about an inch and a half below the lobe below, and about two and a half inches behind the left ear, and extended across the throat to about three inches below the lobe of the right ear.

The big muscle across the throat was divided through on the left side. The large vessels on the left side of the neck were severed. The larynx was severed below the vocal chord. All the deep structures were severed to the bone, the knife marking the intervertebral cartilages. The sheath of the vessels on the right side was just opened.

The carotid artery had a fine hole opening, the internal jugular vein was opened about an inch and a half – not divided. The blood vessels contained clot. All these injuries were performed by a sharp instrument like a knife, and pointed.

The cause of death was hemorrhage from the left common artery. The death was immediate and the mutilations were inflicted after death.

We examined the abdomen. The front walls were laid open from the breast bones to the pubes. The cut commenced opposite the ensiform cartilage. The incision went upwards, not penetrating the skin that was over the sternum. It then divided the ensiform cartilage. The knife must have cut obliquely at the expense of that cartilage.

Behind this, the liver was stabbed as if by the point of a sharp instrument. Below this was another incision into the liver of about two and a half inches, and below this the left lobe of the liver was slit through by a vertical cut. Two cuts were shewn by a jagging of the skin on the left side.

The abdominal walls were divided in the middle line to within a quarter of an inch of the navel. The cut then took a horizontal course for two inches an a half towards the right side. It then divided round the navel on the left side, and made a parallel incision to the former horizontal incision, leaving the navel on a tongue of skin. Attached to the navel was two and a half inches of the lower part of the rectus muscle on the left side of the abdomen. The incision then took an oblique direction to the right and was shelving. The incision went down the right side of the vagina and rectum for half an inch behind the rectum.

There was a stab of about an inch on the left groin. This was done by a pointed instrument. Below this was a cut of three inches going through all tissues making a wound of the peritoneum about the same extent.

An inch below the crease of the thigh was a cut extending from the anterior spine of the ilium obliquely down the inner side of the left thigh and separating the left labium, forming a flap of skin up to the groin. The left rectus muscle was not detached.

There was a flap of skin formed by the right thigh, attaching the right labium, and extending up to the spine of the ilium. The muscles on the right side inserted into the frontal ligaments were cut through.

Jack the Ripper

The skin was retracted through the whole of the cut through the abdomen, but the vessels were not clotted. Nor had there been any appreciable bleeding from the vessels. I draw the conclusion that the act was made after death, and there would not have been much blood on the murderer. The cut was made by someone on the right side of the body, kneeling below the middle of the body.

I removed the content of the stomach and placed it in a jar for further examination. There seemed very little in it in the way of food or fluid, but from the cut end partly digested farinaceous food escaped. The intestines had been detached to a large extent from the mesentery. About two feet of the colon was cut away. The sigmoid flexure was invaginated into the rectum very tightly.

Right kidney was pale, bloodless with slight congestion of the base of the pyramids.

There was a cut from the upper part of the slit on the under surface of the liver to the left side, and another cut at right angles to this, which were about an inch and a half deep and two and a half inches long. Liver itself was healthy.

The gall bladder contained bile. The pancreas was cut, but not through, on the left side of the spinal column. Three and a half inches of the lower border of the spleen by half an inch was attached only to the peritoneum.

The peritoneal lining was cut through on the left side and the kidney carefully taken out and removed. The left renal artery was cut through. I would say that someone who knew the position of the

THE AUTOPSIES

kidney must have done it.

The lining membrane over the uterus was cut through. The womb was cut through horizontally, leaving a stump of three quarters of an inch. The rest of the womb had been taken away with some of the ligaments. The vagina and cervix of the womb was uninjured.

The bladder was healthy and uninjured, and contained three or four ounces of water. There was a tongue like cut through the anterior wall of the abdominal aorta. The other organs were healthy. There were no indications of connexion. I believe the wound in the throat was first inflicted. I believe she must have been lying on the ground.

The wounds on the face and abdomen prove that they were inflicted by a sharp, pointed knife, and that in the abdomen by one six inches or longer.

I believe the perpetrator of the act must have had considerable knowledge of the position of the organs in the abdominal cavity and the way of removing them. It required a great deal of medical knowledge to have removed the kidney and to know where it was placed. The parts removed would be of no use for any professional purpose.

I think the perpetrator of this act had sufficient time, or he would not have nicked the lower eyelids. It would take at least five minutes.

I cannot assign any reason for the parts being taken away. I feel sure that there was no struggle, and believe it was the act of one person.

The throat had been so instantly severed that no noise could have been emitted. I should not expect much blood to have been found on the person who had inflicted these wounds. The wounds could not have been self-inflicted.

My attention was called to the apron, particularly the corner of the apron with a string attached. The blood spots were of recent origin. I have seen the portion of an apron produced by Dr Phillips and stated to have been found in Goulston Street. It is impossible to say that it is human blood on the apron. I fitted the piece of apron, which had a new piece of material on it (which had evidently been sewn on to the piece I have), the seams of the borders of the two actually corresponding. Some blood and apparently faecal matter was found on the portion that was found in Goulston Street.

Mary Kelly

The post mortem was carried out by Dr Thomas Bond of 7 Broad Sanctuary S.W. It was, however, Dr George Bagster Phillips of 2 Spital Square, the police divisional surgeon who had examined the body at the murder scene who appeared at the inquest on 12 November:

The face was gashed in all directions, the nose, cheeks, eyebrows, and ears being partly removed. The lips were blanched and cut by several incisions running obliquely down to the chin. There were also numerous cuts extending irregularly across all the features.

The neck was cut through the skin and other tissues right down to the vertebrae, the fifth and sixth being deeply notched. The skin cuts in the front of the neck showed distinct ecchymosis. The air passage was cut at the lower part of the larynx through the cricoid cartilage.

Both breasts were more or less removed by circular incisions, the muscle down to the ribs being attached to the breasts. The intercostals between the fourth, fifth and sixth ribs were cut through and the contents of the thorax visible through the openings.

The skin and tissues of the abdomen from the costal arch to the pubes were removed in three large flaps. The right thigh was denuded in front to the bone, the flap of skin, including the external organs of generation, and part of the right buttock. The left thigh was stripped of skin fascia, and muscles as far as the knee.

The left calf showed a long gash through skin and tissues to the deep muscles and reaching from the knee to five inches above the ankle. Both arms and forearms had extensive jagged wounds.

The right thumb showed a small superficial incision about one inch long, with extravasation of blood in the skin, and there were several abrasions on the back of the hand moreover showing the same condition.

On opening the thorax it was found that the right lung was minimally adherent by old firm adhesions. The lower part of the lung was broken and torn away. The left lung was intact. It was adherent at the apex and there were several nodules of consolidation.

The pericardium was open below and the heart absent. In the abdominal cavity there was some partly digested food of fish and potatoes, and similar food was found in the remains of the stomach attached to the intestines.

Alice McKenzie

The post mortem was carried out by Dr Bagster Phillips of 2 Spital Square, police divisional surgeon. He reported to the inquest on 14 August:

Condition of Clothing. The clothing was fastened round the body somewhat tightly & could only be raised so as to expose about 1/3 of the abdomen. The back part of the under garment was well saturated with blood stained fluid. Bruises upper part of chest.

Over upon & below the left collar bone there is a well defined bruise about the size of a shilling situate about the junction of the inner 1/3 and outer 2/3 of the collar bone. & on the right side an inch below the sterno clavicular articulation is another larger and more defined bruise most marked at its outer border. Dilated veins. Between the mammaries in middle line of sternum in a direct line downwards with the last named bruise are several congested veins seen through the skin. Scorings & Wounds of Abdomen.

Seven inches below right nipple commences a wound 7 inches long, not quite straight in direction, inclining first inward & then outward, deepest at its upper part and ending below in a subcutaneous dissection possibly 3 or perhaps 4 inches. [*in whole (?)*] abdominal cavity not opened. Scoring on right side.

THE AUTOPSIES

Neither abdominal cavity opened – or muscular covering divided. Tailing toward inner border of this wound are seven dermal marks only dividing the skin & ascending above the deeper incision, and 7 similar scorings descending lower than the major wound. and between it and pubis. One distinct became deeper over the pubis. Marks and blood stains left side. There are 5 small (excoriating) marks below and between umbilicus and pubis some what transverse in direction col red one ¾ in. in length, and the smallest a [?] in length.

Somewhat nearer to the left side there strains of blood surrounding a bruise the size of a fourpenny piece, (& corresponding with scores on right side). The larger marking is the lowest and the smallest nearest the right side. & all of them are 4 in. from prominence of pelvis & 4 in. below umbilicus. Old scars & signs of injury. There are old scars & bruisings over patella front of shins & three distinct cicatrices on Dresum of left forearm. Loss of terminal joint of left thumb from some cutting instrument, which has left half the nail.

Genital signs. There is no sign of Coitus. Syphilitic Condylomata of vagina and ulceration of mucous membrane under clitoris. Congestion Anal external piles & excretion of a small quantity of liquid faeces. Description of wound in neck. More superficial two jagged wounds commence from behind the left sterno mastoid muscle leaving a triangular piece of skin attached by its base to the outside (remaining) skin about an inch long and four inches forward & upwards. Deeper.

The deepest incision divides the Sterno M. muscle except a few posterior fibres. the vessels of the neck & sheath, the division of the Common Carotid being above the Omo hyoid muscle, down to the transverse process of the Cervical Vertebra. There are four jagged cuts over angle of jaw where instrument had been arrested [?] over cut under jaw. No sign of fall backwards.No sign of bruise back of Head or under Scalp. Brain app. and other visceral app. *fairly normal* & healthy. *Brain* healthy but meningel vessels fuller than might have been expected. *Lungs* old adhesions posterior part of right. Left healthy Both well filled with air & not congested. Heart healthy small quantity of fluid in pericardium, colour red, walls good, Valves healthy. Cavities empty and contracted. Large vessels healthy no clots. Liver, fairly healthy rather pale.

Spleen and Kidneys fairly healthy. Stomach large contains rather more than a pint of pultaceous matter which has a faint alcoholic smell. Mucous membrane pale. Bladder contracted and empty. Uterus small. healthy. Unimpregnated. Ovaries contain small cysts. Conclusions. Death was caused through Syncope arising from the division of the vessels of neck left side. Nature of instrument and its use.

The wound was caused by sharp cutting instrument with at least two strokes. was not suicidal, was made from left to right, while the body was on the ground & effected by someone who knew the position of the vessels, at any rate where to cut with reference to causing speedy death. No sign of struggle but of holding down. No sign of violent struggle but of body being held down by hand as evidenced by bruises on upper chest and collar bone. Greater Pressure – right. There was more pressure on the right side. Further conclusions.

No physiological reason why the woman should not have uttered a cry. The wound in the throat tends to confirm the conclusion submitted as to the wounds of the abdominal wall.

That death almost immediately followed the incision of the neck. That the woman did not move after the said incision. The superficial marks on left side of abdomen were characteristic of pressure with a Thumb and Fingers. they compared in position to a right hand placed on the abdomen pinching up a fold of skin for at least 3 inches. That the smearing of blood was caused in this way.

The scoring and cuts of skin on Pubis were caused through the endeavour to pass the obstruction caused by the clothing. The long wound right side of abdomen was inflicted by a sharp pointed instrument from above downwards and (there is evidence of two thrusts of instrument before withdrawal) the instrument turned laterally while making the undermining portion of wound which was made from right to left. Admit that the appearances observed on left side of abdomen were caused by the pressure of a right hand (possibly to facilitate the introduction of an instrument under the (tight) clothing there the right wounds were produced by a left handed cut. The abdominal injuries were caused subsequent to the throat being cut. The instrument used was smaller than the one used in most of the cases that have come under my observation in these "Whitechapel Murders." Concurrence of Dr. G. Brown.

Dr Gordon Brown (city police surgeon) has been good enough to express his concurrence in the foregoing conclusions, but he has not expressed his opinion concerning the following remarks, which have not formally been submitted to him:

On Thursday about 6pm I accompanied Dr. Bond to view the body of Dec'd and so far as I was able explained the appearances to him. Decomposition had fairly begun, though not very markedly. There was great difficulty without again opening up the incisions in giving a description of the appearances – and it appeared to me that the body had been washed since the former examination.

On Saturday last at noon I again in the presence of Dr. Brown re-examined the body for the purpose of demonstrating the appearances on the abdomen. I believe I satisfied him of the correctness of the appearances, and this must be so as he has since signified generally his assent to the report.

After careful and long deliberation I cannot satisfy myself on purely anatomical and professional grounds that the Perpetrator of all the "WhChl.murders" is one man.

I am on the contrary impelled to a contrary conclusion. This noting the mode of procedure and the character of the mutilations and judging of motive in connection with the latter.

Because of the controversy concerning whether or not this was a Ripper murder, a second autopsy was held, this time officiated by Dr Thomas Bond:

I beg to report that in accordance with your instructions I this day inspected the dead body of a woman, who had been identified as Alice McKenzie, at Whitechapel. Before I went to the mortuary I called on Dr. Phillips & he kindly accompanied me. He informed me that the post mortem was completed yesterday & that the wounds on the throat of the woman had been so disturbed that any examination I might make, unassisted would convey no definite information as to the nature of the injuries. He pointed out to me the original wounds, their daughter and direction & I was able to form an opinion that there could be no doubt that the cuts were made from left to right & as far as I was able to make out, the knife appears to have been plunged deeply into the left side of the victim below the sterno mastoid muscle & brought out by a tailed incision just above the larynx on the same side. There appeared to have been two stabs, & the knife then carried forward in the same skin wound, except that a small tongue of skin remained between the two stabs. The incisions appeared to me to be in a direction from above downwards and forwards with several small superficial cuts extending upward & tailing off into mere scratches. The two main cuts appeared to be about 3 inches long but Dr. Phillips stated that before the parts were disturbed the cuts which I saw extending down wards, really were in I direction upwards.

The cuts appeared to have been inflicted with a sharp strong knife. I could form no opinion as to the width of the blade or the length of the knife, but undoubtedly the cuts might have been done with a short knife; it must in my opinion have had a sharp point. I believe the cuts were made from the front while the woman's head was thrown back on the ground. There were two bruises high up on the chest which looked as if the murder had made the cuts with his right hand while he held the woman down with his left. There were no bruises on the woman's face or lips.

On the right side of the abdomen extending from the chest to below the level of the umbilicus there was a jagged incision made up of several cuts which extended through the skin & subcutaneous fat & at the bottom of this cut there were 7 or 8 superficial scratches about 2 inches long parallel to each other in a longitudinal direction. There was also a small cut eighth of an inch deep, quarter inch long on the mons veneris. I think that in order to inflict the wound which I saw on the abdomen the murderer must have raised the clothes with his left hand & inflicted the injuries with his right.

Dr Phillips showed me a small bruise on the left side of the stomach which he suggested might have been caused by the murderer pressing his right hand on the stomach while he used the knife with his left hand, but I saw no sufficient reason to entertain this opinion. The wounds could not have been self inflicted, & no doubt the wound in the throat would cause almost immediate death & I do not think the woman could call out if held down in the position she appears to have been in when the wounds were inflicted. The wounds on the abdomen could have nothing to do with the cause of death and were in my opinion inflicted after death. I see in this murder evidence of similar design to the former Whitechapel murders viz. sudden onslaught on the prostrate woman, the throat skilfully & resolutely cut with subsequent mutilation, each mutilation indicating sexual thoughts & a desire to mutilate the abdomen & sexual organs.

I am of opinion that the murder was performed by the same person who committed the former series of Whitechapel murders.

Francis Coles

The post mortem was carried out by Dr George Bagster Phillips of 2 Spital Square, a police divisional surgeon. He reported the following to the inquest on 23 February:

> On Saturday morning I made a minute examination of the incision in the throat. There was an external wound, the edges of the skin being not exactly cut through, there being a portion of about an inch long undivided. In my opinion, there were three distinct passing of the knife across the throat - one from left to right, one from right to left, and the third from left to right. Below the wound there was an abrasion, as if caused by a finger nail. Above the wound there were four abrasions, possibly caused by finger nails. From the position of these marks I opine that the left hand was used. There were some contused wounds on the back of the head, which I am of opinion were caused by the head coming into violent contact with paving stones. I came to the conclusion that death had been almost instantaneous, occasioned by the severance of the carotid arteries and other vessels on the left side. In my opinion, the deceased was on the ground when her throat was cut. I think that her assailant used his right hand in making the incisions in the throat, and that he had used his left hand to hold her head back by the chin; that he was on the right side of the body when he made the cuts. The tilting of the body to the left was to prevent the perpetrator from being stained with blood. There was a complete absence of any struggle or even any movement from pain, but it may have arisen from the fact that the woman was insensible from concussion. The knife produced would be capable of inflicting all the wounds found on the neck. It was not a very sharp knife that caused the wounds.

SOURCES

BL	British Library
CAB	Cabinet Office (UK)
CLRO	Corporation of London Records Office
DPP	Director of Public Prosecutions
HO	Home Office
FO	Foreign Office
LRO	Liverpool Record Office
LMA	London Metropolitan Archive
MEPO	Metropolitan Police
NRO	Norfolk Record Office
PRO	See TNA
TNA	The National Archive, Kew (formerly Public Record Office)

Preface

Andrew Cook, Cash for Honours, (Sutton Press), 2008
The Lloyd George Papers, Parliamentary Archive, London
Brunner Family Papers
The Asquith Papers, Bodleian Library, Oxford
T.P. O'Connor Family Papers
The T.P. O'Connor Papers (Liverpool Record Office)
T.P. O'Connor, Memoirs of an Old Parliamentarian, (Ernest Benn Ltd), 1929
T.P. O'Connor, Hamilton Fyfe (Allen & Unwin), 1934
The Daily Telegraph; The Sun (British Library Newspaper Library, Colindale)

SOURCES

Chapter 1: With Thanks To Jack The Ripper

Pall Mall Gazette; The Star; The Times; The Daily News; The Morning Advertiser; The Herald; The East London Advertiser (British Library Newspaper Library, Colindale)
T. P. O'Connor Family Papers
The T.P. O'Connor Papers (Liverpool Record Office)
Memoirs of an Old Parliamentarian, Ibid
T. P. O'Connor, Hamilton Fyfe, Ibid
Brunner Family Papers
Records of the Newspaper Publishing Company Ltd (Reg # 24991)

Chapter 2: Murder In Retrospect

Gerald Posner, Case Closed, (Random House), 1993
Sunday Times (British Library Newspaper Library, Colindale)
Metropolitan Police Files on Whitechapel Murders, TNA MEPO 3/140
Whitechapel Murders, miscellaneous correspondence, TNA MEPO 3/141
Report on Miller's Court Murder, TNA HO/144/221/A49301F
Poplar Murder Statement, TNA HO/144/221/A49301H
Police Report on Castle Alley murder, TNA HO/144/221/A49301I
Police Report on Pinchin Street murder, TNA HO/144/221/A49301K

Chapter 3: Hang Leather Apron

The Star; The Times; Daily Telegraph (British Library Newspaper Library, Colindale)
Metropolitan Police Files on murders, TNA MEPO 3/140
Report on endeavours to trace criminal, TNA HO/144/221/A49301C
The Papers of T.P. O'Connor (Liverpool Record Office)
The Family Papers of T.P. O'Connor

Chapter 4: Dear Boss

Derby Mercury; The Star; The Evening News; The East Anglian Times; Sunderland Post; Daily Telegraph (British Library Newspaper Library, Colindale)
The Brunner Family Papers

Records of the Newspaper Publishing Company Ltd (Reg # 24991)

The Massingham Family Papers

The Henry Massingham Papers (Norfolk Record Office)

The Ernest Parke Papers (Liverpool Record Office)

Hansard, Parliamentary Archive, (London)

Records of Central News Ltd (Reg # 14404)

'Jack the Ripper' Letters, TNA MEMO 3/142

Walter Dew (Blackie & Son), I Caught Crippen, 1938

Stewart P Evans and Keith Skinner, Jack the Ripper: Letters from Hell, (Sutton), 2001

Chapter 5: The Hidden Hand

The Referee; Daily Telegraph, Independent (British Library Newspaper Library, Colindale)

Sir Robert Anderson, The Lighter Side of My Life, (Hodder & Stoughton), 1910

Sir Melville Macnaghten, Days of My Years, (Edward Arnold), 1914

Andrew Cook, M: MI5's First Spymaster, (Tempus), 2004

Stewart P. Evans and Paul Gainey, The Lodger, (Century), 1995

Records of Central News Ltd (Reg # 14404)

Bulling Family Records

Moore Family Records

R. Thurston Hopkins, Life and Death at the Old Bailey, (Herbert Jenkins), 1935

Report by Elaine Quigley on the 'Dear Boss' Letter for 'Jack the Ripper: Tabloid Killer', Channel 5, 2009

Best Family Records

US Immigration Records; 1880/1889, US Department of Labor

Stewart P Evans and Keith Skinner, Jack the Ripper: Letters from Hell, (Sutton), 2001

Chapter 6: Cannibal Ripper

The Star; Evening News; Manchester Evening News; Daily Telegraph (British Library Newspaper Library, Colindale)

Constable to Commissioner, Sir Henry Smith (Chatto & Windus), 1910

Coroner's inquest (L), 1888, No135, Catherine Eddowes inquest, 1888, CLRO

SOURCES

Commissioner's Letters 1867-1891, TNA MEPO 1/48
Letters to the Home Office 1883-1904, TNA MEPO 1/55
Metropolitan Police files on murders, MEPO 3/140

Chapter 7: Copy Cat Killers

Metropolitan Police files on murders, TNA MEMO 3/140
Sir Melville Macnaghton, Days of My Years, (Edward Arnold), 1914
The Papers of Sir Basil Thomson
Interview with Thomas Arnold, East London Observer, 20 May 1893
Interview with Thomas Arnold, Eastern Post & City Chronicle, 4 February 1893
Interview with Dr Percy Clark, East London Observer, 14 May 1910
Daily Telegraph, The Times; East London Observer; Eastern Post & City Chronicle (British Library Newspaper Library, Colindale)
Metropolitan Police files on murders, TNA MEPO 3/140
Report on endeavours to trace criminal, TNA/HO 144/221/49301C
Report on Miller's Court murder, TNA/HO 144/221/ 49301F
Coroner's inquest (L), 1888, No 135, Catherine Eddowes inquest, 1888, CLRO
Mary Jane Kelly inquest, MJ/SPC, NE1888, Box 3, Case Paper 19, LMA
Dr Bond 'profiles' the Killer, TNA HO 144/221/A49301C

Chapter 8: A Process of Elimination

Evening News; Daily Telegraph; Daily News; Police Gazette; Weekly Dispatch (British Library Newspaper Library, Colindale)
Report by Chief Inspector D. Swanson, 19 October 1888, TNA HO 144/221/ A49301C
Report by Inspector F. Abberline, 1 November 1888, TNA MEPO 3/140/221/ A49301C
Statement by George Hutchinson, 12 November 1888, TNA MEPO 3/140/227-9
Report by Inspector Abberline, 12 November 1888, TNA MEPO 3/140 /230-2
Susan Kelly, The Boston Stranglers, (Citadel), 1995
The Boston Strangler, 48 Hours Mystery, 15 February 200-1, CBS News
Casey Sherman and Dick Lehr, A Rose for Mary: The Hunt for the Boston Strangler, (North Eastern University Press), 2003

Chapter 9: The Mask of Sanity

Interview with Dr Percy Clark, East London Observer, 14 May 1910
Interview with former Inspector Edmund Reid, Morning Advertiser, 23 April 1910
Morning Advertiser; The Star; The East London Advertiser (British Library Newspaper Library, Colindale)
Report by Dr George Bagster Phillips, 22 July 1889, TNA MEPO 3/140/263-71
1891, 1901, 1911 UK Census
Passenger List 1890-1960, Board of Trade, Archives D3, TNA
US Immigration Records, US Department of Labor
Probate Records, Merced County, California
Report of Professor Derrick Pounder for 'Jack the Ripper: Tabloid Killer', Channel 5, 2009
Hervey M Cleckley, The Mask of Sanity, (Mosby), 1941

Chapter 10: Journey's End

T.P. O'Connor Family Papers
Records of the Newspaper Publishing Company Ltd (Ref # 24991)
Records of the Star Newspaper Company Ltd (Ref# 31973)
T.P. O'Connor, Memoirs of an Old Parliamentarian, (Ernest Benn Ltd), 1929
Brunner Family Papers
The Massingham Family Papers
Broadmoor files (3) on Thomas H Cutbush (Reg # X32007), Broadmoor Hospital, Berkshire
Interview with Dr Percy Clark, East London Observer, 14 May 1910
The Papers of Dr Percy Clark
The Sun; East London Observer (British Library Newspaper Library, Colindale)

BIBLIOGRAPHY

Abrahamsen, David, *Murder & Madness,* London, Robson Books, 1992

Ambler, Eric, *The Ability to Kill and Other Pieces,* London, The Bodley Head, 1963

Anderson, Sir Robert, K.C.B., *The Lighter Side of My Official Life,* London, Hodder & Stoughton, 1910

Beaumont, F.A., 'The Fiend of East London', in *The Fifty Most Amazing Crimes of the last 100 Years,* London, Odhams, 1936

Begg, Paul, Fido, Martin and Skinner, Keith, *The Jack the Ripper A-Z,* London, Headline, 1996 (revised paperback)

Bernard, Allen (ed.), *The Harlot Killer, Jack the Ripper,* New York, Mead & Co 1953

Boyce, D.G. (ed), *Newspaper History: From the Seventeenth Century to the Present Day,* London, Constable, 1978

Brady, L W, *T.P. O'Connor and the Liverpool Irish,* Royal Historical Society Study Studies in History, 1984

Browne, Douglas G., *The Rise of Scotland Yard: A History of the Metropolitan Police,* London, Harrap, 1956

Butler, Ivan, *Murderers' London,* London, Robert Hale, 1973

Campbell, Christy, *Fenian Fire,* London, Harper Collins, 2002

Cargill, David and Holland, Julian, *Scenes of Murder: A London Guide,* London, Heinemann, 1964

Chibnall, Steve, *Law and Order News: An Analysis of Crime Reporting in the British Press,* London, Tavistock Publications, 1977

Clarke, Bob, *From Grubb Street to Fleet Street: An Illustrated*

History of English Newspapers to 1899, London, Ashgate, 2004

Cleckley, Hervey, *The Mask of Sanity*, St Louis, C.V. Mosby Company, 1941

Cobb, Belton, *Critical Years at the Yard: The Career of Frederick Williamson of the Detective Department and the C.I.D.*, London, Faber & Faber, 1956

Cook, Andrew, *m: MI5's First Spymaster*, Stroud, Tempus, 2004

Cook, Andrew, *Cash for Honours*, Stroud, Sutton, 2008

Cullen, Tom, *Autumn of Terror – Jack the Ripper: His Crimes & Times*, London, Bodley Head, 1965

Curtis, L. Perry, *Jack the Ripper and the London Press*, New Haven and London Yale University Press, 2001

Dearden, Harold, 'Who Was Jack the Ripper?' in *Great Unsolved Crimes*, London, Hutchinson, 1935

Dew, ex-Chief Inspector Walter, *I Caught Crippen*, London, Blackie & Sons, 1938

Douthwaite, Louis, *Mass Murder*, London, Long, 1928

Downie, Robert A., *Murder in London – A Topographical Guide to Famous Crimes*, London, Barker, 1973

Eckley, Grace, *Maiden Tribute: A Life of W.T. Stead*, Xlibris, 2007

Evans, Stewart P. and Skinner, Keith, *The Ultimate Jack the Ripper Sourcebook*, London, Constable & Robinson, 2000

Evans, Stewart P, and Skinner, Keith, *Jack the Ripper: Letters from Hell*, Stroud, Sutton, 2001

Evans, Stewart P, and Gainey, Paul, *The Lodger*, London, Century, 1995

Evans, Stewart P, and Rumbellow, Donald, *Jack the Ripper: Scotland Yard Investigates*, Stroud, Sutton, 2006

Evans, Stewart P, and Connell, Nicholas, *The Man Who Hunted the Ripper*, Cambridge, Rupert Books, 2000

Farson, Daniel, *Jack the Ripper*, London, Michael Joseph, 1972

Feldman, Paul H., *Jack the Ripper: The Final Chapter*, London, Virgin, 1997

Fido, Martin, *The Crimes, Detection & Death of Jack the Ripper*, London, Weidenfeld & Nicolson, 1987

Fyfe, Hamilton, *T.P. O'Connor*, London, George Allen & Unwin, 1934

BIBLIOGRAPHY

Griffiths, Major Arthur, *Mysteries of Police and Crime*, 2 volumes, London, Cassell, 1898

Harris, Melvin, *The Ripper File*, London, W.H. Allen, 1989

Harris, Melvin, *Jack the Ripper The Bloody Truth*, London, Columbus Books, 1987

Harris, Melvin, *The True Face of Jack the Ripper*, London, Michael O'Mara, 1994

Harris, Michael and O'Malley, Tom, (eds), *Studies in Newspaper and Periodical History*, London, Greenwood Press, (revised and updated) 1997

Hopkins, R. Thurston, *Life and Death at the Old Bailey*, London, Herbert Jenkins, 1935

Howells. Martin, and Skinner, Keith, *The Ripper Legacy*, London, Sidgwick & Jackson,1987

Jones, Aled, *Powers of the Press: Newspapers, Power and the Public in Nineteenth Century England*, Aldershot, 1996

Jones, Elwyn and Lloyd, John, *The Ripper File*, London, Arthur Barker, 1975

Jones, Victor, *Saint or Sensationalist? The Story of W.T .Stead*, London, Gooday, 1988

Keith, Williams, *The English Newspaper: An Illustrated History to 1900*, London, Springwood, 1977

Knight, Stephen, *Jack the Ripper: The Final Solution*, London, Harrap, 1976

Koss, Stephen, *Sir John Brunner: Radical Plutocrat*, Cambridge, Cambridge University Press, 1970

Koss, Stephen, *Rise and Fall of the Political Press, Vol. 1*, Chapel Hill, 1981

Lake, Brian, *British Newspapers: A History and Guide for Collectors*, London, Sheppard, 1984

Lansdowne, Andrew, *A Life's Reminiscences of Scotland Yard*, London, Leadenhall Press, 1890

Lee, Alan, *The Origins of the Popular Press in England*, Rowman & Littlefield, 1976

Logan, Guy B.H., 'The Ripper Murders', in *Masters of Crime*, London, Stanley Paul, 1928

Macleod, C.M., 'A "Ripper" Handwriting Analysis',
The Criminologist, No. 9, August 1968

Macnaughten, Sir Melville L., CB, *Days of My Years,* London Edward Arnold, 1914

Mccormick, Donald, *The Identity of Jack the Ripper,* London, Jarrolds, 1959 and revised edition, 1970

Macnaughten. Sir Melville, *Days of My Years,* London, Edward Arnold, 1914

Massingham, H. J., *A Selection from the Writings of H.J. Massingham,* London, J. Cape, 1925

Massingham, H.J., *Letters to X,* London, Constable, 1919

Matters, Leonard, *The Mystery of Jack the Ripper,* London, Hutchinson, 1929 (reprinted W.H. Allen, 1948)

Moore-Anderson, A.P., *Sir Robert Anderson K.C.B. L.L.D. and Lady Agnes Anderson,* London, Marshall, Morgan & Scott, 1947

O'Connor, T.P., *The New Journalism, New Review Vol1, No5 (October 1889, p. 423-434)*

O'Connor, T.P., *Memoirs of an Old Parliamentarian, 2 Volumes,* London, Ernest Benn, 1929

Odell, Robin, *Jack the Ripper in Fact and Fiction,* London, Harrap, 1965

Porter, Bernard, *The Origins of the Vigilant State: The London Metropolitan Police*

Special Branch before the First World War, London, Weidenfeld & Nicolson, 1987

Prothero, Margaret, *The History of the Criminal Investigation Department at Scotland*

Yard, London, Herbert Jenkins, 1931

Richardson, J. Hall, *From the City to Fleet Street,* London, Stanley Paul, 1927

Robertson Scott, J.W., *The Life & Death of a Newspaper,* London, Methuen, 1952

Rumbellow, Donald, *The Complete Jack the Ripper,* London, Penguin, (revised paperback), 2004

Sharkey, Terence, *Jack the Ripper – 100 Years of Investigation,* London, Ward Lock, 1987

Short, K.R.M., *The Dynamite War: Irish-American Bombers in Victorian Britain,* Dublin, Gill & Macmillan, 1979

Shrew, Edward Spencer, *A Companion to Murder,* London, Cassell, 1960

Simonis, H., *The Streets of Ink,* London, Cassell, 1917

Sims, George R., *Mysteries of Modern London,* London, C. Arthur Person, 1906

Smith, Lt-Col Sir Henry, K.C.B., *From Constable to Commissioner,*

BIBLIOGRAPHY

London, Chatto & Windus, 1910

Stewart, William, *Jack the Ripper – A New Theory*, Quality Press, 1939

Sweeney, John, (ed. By Francis Richards), *At Scotland Yard: Being the experiences during twenty-seven years service of John Sweeney Late Detective Inspector, Criminal Investigation Department, New Scotland Yard*, London, Grant Richards, 1904

Sugden, Philip, *The Complete History of Jack the Ripper*, London, Robinson, 1995 (revised paperback)

Sugden, Philip, *The Complete History of Jack the Ripper*, London, Robinson, 1994

Thomson, Sir Basil, *My Experiences at Scotland Yard*, New York, Doubleday & Doran, 1923

Thomson, Sir Basil, *The Story of Scotland Yard*, London, Grayson & Grayson, 1935

Underwood, Peter, *Jack the Ripper – One Hundred Years of Mystery*, Blandford Press, 1987

Waddell, Bill, *The Black Museum*, London, Little, Brown, 1993

Wadsworth, A. P., *Newspaper Circulations 1800-1954*, Manchester Statistical Society, 1954

Walbeck, H. M., *Life and Death at the Old Bailey*, Herbert Jenkins, London, Constable, 1935

Walbrook, H. M., *Murders and Murder Trials 1812-1912*, London, Constable, 1932

Warwick, Alexandra & Willis, Martin, *Jack the Ripper, Media, Culture and History*, Manchester, Manchester University Press, 2007

Whittington-Egan, Molly, *Doctor Forbes Winslow, Defender of the Insane*, Great Malvern, Cappella Archive, 2000

Williams, Watkin W., *The Life of General Sir Charles Warren*, Oxford, Basil Blackwell, 1941

Wilson, Colin, *A Casebook for Murder, London*, Leslie Frewin, 1969

Winslow, L. Forbes, MB, DCL, LLD, *Recollections of Forty Years*, London, John Ouseley, 1910

Wolf, A. P., *Jack the Myth*, Hale, 1993

Wolff, Camille (compiled by), *Who Was Jack the Ripper?*, Grey House Books, 1995

Wynne-Jones, Michael, *A Newspaper History of the World: An Anthology of famous news stories from 1850 to the present day*, New York, Morrow, 1974

ACKNOWLEDGEMENTS

First may I thank Bill Locke at Lion Television (Executive Producer of the TV film *Jack the Ripper: Tabloid Killer*) whose unstinting support and encouragement enabled me to take this project forward. I am also indebted to Hannah Beckerman at Channel 5 for commissioning this story thus enabling the new research surrounding the fabrication and creation of the Jack the Ripper myth to be presented to a wider public. Thanks must also go to all those involved in the production of the film, in particular Nicki Stoker, Jack MacInnes and Kelvin McKenzie for their part in making it such a powerful and thought-provoking film.

I am also greatly indebted to the families and heirs of Frederick Best, Sir John Brunner, Thomas Bulling, Dr Percy Clark, Henry Massinghan, John Moore, T.P. O'Connor and Ernest Parke.

My thanks go to the following individuals who greatly assisted with various aspects of research during the making of the TV documentary and for this book; Bill Adams, Jordan Auslander, Phil Tomaselli, Professor Derrick Pounder, Elaine Quigley and the staff at the National Archive in Kew.

A very much appreciated thank you in particular to Stewart P. Evans, for allowing access to his unique collection of photographs and documents and for his thoughts and opinions throughout the writing of this book. As one of the few objective, evidence based researchers in this field, his assistance and advice was invaluable.

A special thank you also goes to Siobhan Casson, Daksha Chauhan, David Cook, Sonia Dipaolo, Tammie Elliott, Julia Edwards, Linda Griggs, Helen Kaltio and Nina Kalyan for their assistance in the production of the book. Finally, my thanks go to Jonathan Reeve at Amberley Publishing who inspired the theme of the book and supported the project throughout.

LIST OF ILLUSTRATIONS

1. Mortuary photo of Martha Tabram.
2. Mortuary photo of Mary Ann Nichols.
3. Mortuary photo of Annie Chapman; the *Star* claimed she was the third victim of a maniac.
4. Mortuary photo of Elizabeth Stride; already the doctors were doubting that she had been murdered by the same hand as Chapman.
5. Elizabeth Stride: An contemporary artist's impression of Elizabeth Stride in life
6. Catherine Eddowes after the post mortem stitching.
7. Catherine Eddowes' facial mutilations can be better seen in this close up.
8. Catherine Eddowes before the post mortem, the chest cavity and throat wounds are still open.
9. A contemporary artist's impression of Catherine Eddowes in life.
10. A rarely seen contemporary artist's impression of Kelly in life.
11. The murder scene at 13 Miller's Court; Kelly's virtually unrecognisable body lays on the bed.
12. A mortuary photo of Alice McKenzie, her copycat murder was so similar to Nichols and Chapman, some though, she was killed by the same man.
13. A mortuary photo of Frances Coles; the police initially believed she was a victim of the Ripper.
14. An artist's impression of the discovery of Martha Tabram's body; she was most likely murdered by a soldier client.
15. PC John Neil shines his bulldog lamp on the body of Mary Ann Nichols in Bucks Row.
16. 29 Hanbury Street; Annie Chapman's body was found in the back yard.
17. A rarely seen interior view of 29 Hanbury Street. Chapman and her murderer would have passed through here and out the back door to

the yard.

18. Berner Street; the gates to Dutfield's Yard is below the cartwheel.

19. Louis Diemschutz discovers Elizabeth Strides body just inside the gates of Dutfield's yard.

20. Crowds gathering at the murder scene outside Dutfield's Yard.

21. Goulston Street; the murderer threw down part of Eddowes' apron in this doorway, but did he stop to write the graffiti?

22. Artist's impression of where Eddowes' body was found in Mitre Square.

23. Mitre Square showing the entrance from Mitre Street, X marks the spot of the murder.

24. A rarely seen illustration of the interior of 13 Miller's Court.

25. The window through which Thomas Bowyer first saw the sickening sight of Mary Kelly's body.

26. Exterior of 26 Dorset Street shortly before it was demolished in 1928.

27. An artist's impression of the man described by George Hutchinson;

28. Joseph Lawende had the closest view of Eddowes' murderer when he passed the couple at the top of Church Passage. Within minutes Eddowes would be dead.

29. Joseph Barnett, one of Mary Kelly's male friends and a possible suspect.

30. Michael Kidney, Elizabeth Stride's abusive partner. She had him charged with assault in 1887.

31. A note from T.P. O'Connor.

32. A note from Ernest Parke's *Star* memo pad.

33. In Brunner's letter to Henry Massingham he refers to his unhappiness over the 'Best' episode.

34. Ernest Parke, the feature writer who crafted the *Star's* Ripper stories.

35. Henry Massingham, Assistant Editor of the *Star* and the man who aided the proprietors in removing O'Connor from the helm.

36. T.P. O'Connor, the creator of the 'single serial killer' and the greatest newspaper headline of all time; 'Jack the Ripper'.

37. John Brunner, one the *Star's* proprietors who eventually lost patience with O'Connor's 'vulgar journalism'.

38. Thomas Bulling's covering note to Scotland Yard which accompanied the 'Dear Boss' letter.

39. The 'Dear Boss' letter was quickly followed by a postcard from the same writer.

40. The 'From Hell' letter to George Lusk which accompanied the half kidney. Was it a medical student's prank?

41. The Whitechapel Murder files at Scotland Yard, prior to their public release and transfer to the National Archive.

42. A contemporary list of the Whitechapel murder victims.

Illustrations 5, 9, 19, 20, 26, 29, 30, 31, 32, 33, 34, 35, 36, 37, 46, 47, 48, 49, 50, 51, 52, 53: author's collection.

Illustrations 1, 2, 3, 4, 6, 7, 8, 11, 12, 13, 14, 15, 16, 18, 21, 22, 23, 24, 25, 27, 28, 40, 41, 42, 44, 45: The Evans/Skinner Crime Archive.

Figures

1. – 47. Details from various letters. Author's collection and Elaine Quigley.

INDEX

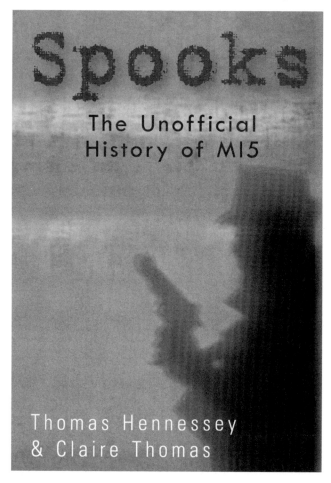

Also available from Amberley Publishing

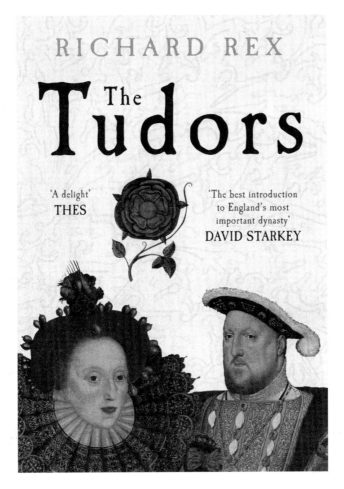

An intimate history of England's most infamous royal family

'The best introduction to England's most important dynasty' DAVID STARKEY
'A lively overview... Rex is a wry commentator on the game on monarchy' THE GUARDIAN
'Gripping and told with enviable narrative skill. This is a model of popular history... a delight' THES
'Vivid, entertaining and carrying its learning lightly' EAMON DUFFY

The Tudor Age began in August 1485 when Henry Tudor landed with 2000 men at Milford Haven intent on snatching the English throne from Richard III. For more than a hundred years England was to be dominated by the personalities of the five Tudor monarchs, ranging from the brilliance and brutality of Henry VIII to the shrewdness and vanity of the virgin queen, Elizabeth I.

£16.99 Paperback
100 colour illustrations
320 pages
978-1-84868-049-4

Available from all good bookshops or to order direct
please call **01285-760-030**

Also available from Amberley Publishing

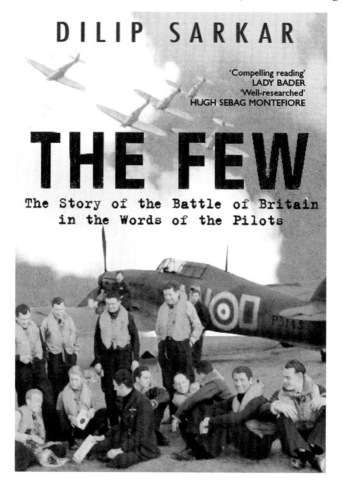

DILIP SARKAR

'Compelling reading'
LADY BADER
'Well-researched'
HUGH SEBAG MONTEFIORE

THE FEW

The Story of the Battle of Britain
in the Words of the Pilots

The history of the Battle of Britain in the words of the pilots

'Over the last 30 years Dilip Sarkar has sought out and interviewed or corresponded with numerous survivors worldwide. Many of these were not famous combatants, but those who formed the unsung backbone of Fighter Command in 1940. Without Dilip's patient recording and collation of their memories, these survivors would not have left behind a permanent record.' LADY BADER
'A well-researched, detailed chronicle of the Battle of Britain' HUGH SEBAG MONTEFIORE
'Dilip knows more about me and the pilots with whom I flew during the Battle of Britain than we do! If anyone ever needs to know anything about the RAF during the summer of 1940, don't ask the Few, ask him!'
GEORGE 'GRUMPY' UNWIN, *Battle of Britain fighter ace*
'Authoritative, lively and deeply touching' PETER TOWNSEND, *Battle of Britain fighter ace*

£20 Hardback
100 photographs
336 pages
978-1-84868-215-3

Available from all good bookshops or to order direct
please call **01285-760-030**